THE GOLDEN FLEECE

The newspaper clipping in the photograph reads:

1965

Navy's Mascot Still Missing

ANNAPOLIS, Md. (P) — The Naval Academy expressed confidence Monday that its missing goat will be returned before the end of the Army-Navy football game Nov. 27.

The goat, mascot for the Navy team, was reported missing early Sunday from its pen on Navy property across the Severn River from the Naval Academy.

A Navy spokesman said academy officials had no details on the circumstances under which the goat disappeared.

He expressed doubt about one report which said eight Cadets from the U. S. Military Academy took the goat Saturday night after using four girls to distract guards by pretending they were lost and asking for directions.

"We don't feel it was done by Cadets," said the academy spokesman.

Courtesy Deme Clainos.

TOM CARHART

The GOLDEN FLEECE

High-Risk Adventure at West Point

Foreword by WESLEY CLARK

Potomac Books

An imprint of the University of Nebraska Press

© 2017 by Tom Carhart

All rights reserved. Potomac Books is an imprint of the
University of Nebraska Press.
Manufactured in the United States of America.

⊗

Library of Congress Control Number: 2017944413

Set in Garamond Premier Pro by Rachel Gould.

That which does not kill us makes us stronger.
—Friedrich Nietzsche

Contents

Foreword

WESLEY CLARK

Over thirty years ago a young *Washington Post* reporter chose to write a compelling memoir of young men in an officer's school, their wartime experiences in Vietnam, and their lives afterward. Who were these men who served and fought in an unpopular, deeply divisive war, and how did their experiences affect them? It was the story of the West Point Class of 1966, called *The Long Gray Line*, by Pulitzer Prize–winning author Rick Atkinson.

Now, long after that class of 579 graduated—most commissioned in the army, a few in the air force or navy—their story is almost told. All but 3 of the army officers served in Vietnam, where 30 died and many times that number were wounded. After the war many left the service and went on to other careers. Today, in their mid-seventies, most of this group have retired from those careers. Among the class were fabulously successful businessmen, entrepreneurs, noted jurists, many successful local and community leaders, educators, academicians, and a number of colonels and generals.

The lessons and meaning of their lives are just now truly coming into focus. Perhaps the most compelling of these lessons is "character": how idealistic, talented young people are shaped by the challenges, pressures, and restraints of a hierarchical and authoritarian institution, and particularly how they blossom with poise, creativity, and courage to face their futures.

Tom Carhart, whose story featured prominently in *The Long Gray Line*, takes us deep into his own life and the lives of other members of that class, as they planned, plotted, and succeeded in stealing Navy's heavily guarded mascot, the Navy goat, just prior to the annual Army-Navy football game. It is a story rich with the particulars of the time—the "Leave it to Beaver" wholesomeness of the generation whose childhood was infused with Walt Disney, Mickey Mantle, and the "dull" presidency of another West Point graduate named Dwight Eisenhower. Theirs was a generation just beginning to experience the openness and rebellion of the sixties. These men faced the growing recognition that they would soon be thrust into a life- and-death struggle in the war in Vietnam.

This is also a timeless story of the path to adulthood—breaking the bonds of parental restriction while also taking risks, all in the pursuit of lofty aims and glory. Long ago Apollonius of Rhodes mythologized the quest for adulthood in the timeless story of Jason and the Golden Fleece: a young man must leave home and risk his life in a distant land to capture the magical wool that will make him king. He uses guile and charm and daring, escaping near-certain death, to ultimately succeed.

Ironically, this is virtually the same story, as Tom and his band of brother Argonauts penetrate the foreign and hostile grounds of the U.S. Naval Academy to steal its famed mascot. But this is a true story, and they succeeded against long odds and high risks. The men involved built on the success of their quest and it became the nugget of each of their life stories: success against the odds but achieved through smart planning, risk-taking, and perseverance.

For the rest of our class the theft was one of those moments that flashed across our lives. We applauded, we gloated a little, we shared in the triumph of our classmates. We sensed at the time that this was no mere prank—it was a classic small-unit military operation done in defiance of our own chain of command. We also sensed that it spoke to some special qualities of our classmates who pulled it off—as the record of their later accomplishments shows. Many of us, no doubt, wished we had had the imagination and daring to be a part of that effort, and perhaps vicariously we absorbed bits of the lesson ourselves.

Gen. Douglas MacArthur, while serving as West Point's superintendent in 1922, expressed it this way: "On the fields of friendly strife are sown the seeds that on other days, on other battlefields, will yield the fruits of victory." So it has been, for this group of men. Read their story, beautifully told by my classmate and friend, Tom Carhart.

I

SPNSS, 0010 Hours, 21 November 1965

I shivered involuntarily, my scalp prickling in the frigid breeze that washed over the back of my head. All five of us were cold, shivering and blowing and stamping our feet silently on the bed of pine needles, restless wild horses while we waited.

Off to our left, a half-dozen high-security communication towers soared 250 feet into the sky, each studded with flashing red lights. It was an eerie sight, as they looked for all the world like a row of rocket ships ready to blast off into space. Off to our right, a few hundred yards down a grassy slope and bathed in a halo of floodlights, was the main guardhouse that blocked the gate into the most secure section of the Severna Park Naval Security Station (SPNSS), Maryland.

It was a moonless night, and we knew that, at the edge of the wood line, we couldn't be seen from the road or the guardhouse. But we also knew we were already trespassers inside the barbed-wire-topped fence of the highest security installation in the U.S. Navy. We were at that moment already in violation of federal law, and we had been warned that if we were seen by either of the U.S. Marine guards stationed at the guardhouse, they had orders to shoot to kill.

We never really believed that, but that's what we had been told by Mr. Acton, the anxious father of one of our number who happened to live nearby. He also told us the story of some teenagers who, weeks earlier and wanting to test the stories going around about this installation, had intentionally thrown a golf ball over the fence, just to see what might happen.

To their great surprise, a voice over a loudspeaker warned them that whatever they had just thrown had violated a federal security installation, that they would not be able to recover it, that they should keep their distance from the high electrified fence and stay where they were until U.S. Marine guards approached them to investigate.

The kids ran, of course, but word went around about that moment, and somehow had been, we thought, exaggerated to include the "shoot to kill" comment. We had talked about this in the Acton home. Mr. Acton's son was our West Point classmate Adam Acton, who had started as part of our group, and I could understand his not wanting his son to run any foolish risks. But, we had argued, we are at peace now, not at war, and they're not going to shoot at us for being little more than "off limits" if we went inside the fence. That seemed like pretty common sense to us, and four of us had been able to talk the others into carrying off this proposed raid. Relax, we said, that threat is almost laughable, they're not going to shoot at us.

But at the last minute, Adam Acton and Billy Blake, another of our classmates, had agreed that the danger was just too great and so had backed out and stayed at the Acton house, leaving the other six of us to conduct our raid. And now, having already violated federal law by penetrating the security station's fence and waiting in the frigid dark, I was of a somewhat more sober mien and began to rethink my words.

Will they shoot at us? Really?

All five of us were wearing jeans and dark turtlenecks, our white hands and faces smeared black by the burnt cork we had rubbed on them before we left the car, its big engine still running with our sixth co-conspirator, Bob Lowry, at the wheel. And now, having come this far, we had long passed the point of no return. We had to make our strike fast and furious, then get back through the fence to the car with our prize. But time dragged while we waited.

Off to my right was Art Mosley, to my left Deme Clainos, Mike Mewhinney, and Mike Brennan. Clainos had a black towel and a small crowbar, maybe two feet long and a half-inch in diameter. But this was supposed to be a backup tool to break the padlock securing the cage, as our primary tool was a big set of bolt cutters we had borrowed from the Post Engineers back at West Point. Their two handles were painted black, but each arm ended with a shiny brass ball the size of a tangerine. And on one arm "Property Corps of Engineers West Point" was stenciled in small white letters.

When we had reached this final rally point only minutes earlier, we checked our equipment: lassoes, check; crowbar, check; (black) towel to muffle the sound of breaking lock, check. But somehow, I had forgotten the bolt cutters. I remembered having them earlier, but for the life of me couldn't remember where I had put them. Were they in the trunk of the car, where they had been earlier? I had no recollection of putting them there, but that was their most probable location.

I admitted my error, but we agreed that if I ran back there and looked for them in the trunk, that could take twenty minutes or so. In any case, we weren't even sure they were there, and we didn't have that much time to spare. No, we couldn't afford any delay, as the arrival of another car at the gate within minutes would be our launch signal. We quickly agreed to just press on and hope that five of us pulling down on the crowbar would provide enough leverage to break the padlock.

The main guardhouse was bathed in a bright pool of light, but we were then inside the fence and looking at it from the rear. There was no activity we could detect, and on the back side of the small brick building, on our side, we could see a large square area no more than twenty feet on a side and enclosed by a Cyclone fence topped with barbed wire. Inside that we could just make out what looked like a small hut. That, we knew, was the cage in which the Navy goat, Billy XIV, was kept, and he was probably inside the hut sleeping.

I checked my watch, which read 12:15. It was a cold Saturday night—or by then, Sunday morning—and we knew that two uniformed Marines manned the well-lit guard post. But while we had watched for ten or fifteen minutes, the Marines just stayed inside. The road through the fence was blocked at the guard post by a big metal barrier whose movement was obviously controlled from inside.

As we watched, one car drove up to the barrier and stopped as one of the Marines came out and checked his pass. Then the barrier was swept back, the car drove in, and the barrier was replaced. That car drove past us no more than fifty feet away, but obviously the driver had no idea we were even there. It seemed strange that there would be any traffic this late on a Saturday night, but we knew nothing of what went on inside all those buildings. We only suspected that it was something very classified that went on day and night, given the high-security nature of the installation.

It seemed almost funny, as the only threat we could imagine to this well-guarded post would be a Soviet agent of some sort. But nothing like that had ever happened, or if it had, he or she must have had very good phony ID. So it was not an enviable position for those poor Marines, pulling the graveyard shift on a cold, lonely Saturday night in November.

I shivered and stamped in the cold, then blew on my hands. It was 12:25 a.m., and the car was expected to arrive any minute. I looked over at Mike Brennan on my left and started to ask him something when Mosley hit my arm as his loud whisper turned my head:

"Here they come!"

Sure enough, a station wagon was rolling into the halo of light, then stopping as it drew close to the barrier.

Brennan's words came in a harsh whisper: "Let's go!"

As one, we dashed out of the woods and swooped down the grassy slope toward the light, our feet only barely touching the ground.

2

High Aspirations

On July 1, 1962, Art Mosley's flight landed at New York's LaGuardia Airport. Having just graduated from high school in Panama City in the panhandle of Florida, Art was, by virtually any high school standard, a bit of a hotshot: number one in his class (he had never gotten a grade lower than "A"), he was also student body president and a star player on his high school baseball team. He was just the sort of high-performing, well-rounded teenager who could have gone to any college in the country.

So where would Art go? He and his father, the chairman of the local school board, had done a lot of research into American colleges over the past year. And which one did they decide was the best? Not Harvard, Yale, or Princeton, not Stanford, not MIT. No, the school they decided would provide the very best education available for Art was the U.S. Military Academy at West Point, New York. And on that first day of July 1962, that's where he was headed.

Another flight to LaGuardia that day would be carrying Mike Mewhinney, from Denton, Texas. He was another very smart guy—National Honor Society and National Merit Scholar, he was also president of his high school student council and played both basketball and baseball. His father had retired from the navy when he was a teenager and was teaching economics at North Texas State University. Mike had the brains and the scholastic aptitude scores to have gone to any college in the country, and he had won an academic scholarship to Rice University, a top-ranked college nationally.

But Mike was the third of five children, and he was well aware that his parents just could not afford much in the way of providing him a college education. With that knowledge, he had applied to his local congressman for an appointment to West Point. When he won, the free education it promised would solve a lot of financial problems at home.

But Mike had never before flown in an airplane, and when he got to Love Field in Dallas, he was more than a little bit nervous, tasting acid in his throat as he tried not to think about it. They got to the gate, where he kissed his parents goodbye, showed his ticket to the guy behind the desk, and was waved out the door. Then they were walking toward the biggest airplane Mike had ever seen, a DC-7 Super Constellation. This was really happening, he thought; he was about to leap into the sky inside this long metal tube with huge wings and long propeller blades.

He found his seat by the window and buckled his seat belt. They stopped briefly at the end of the runway, then the motors roared, the brakes were released, and they accelerated faster than anything Mike had ever experienced, pressing him back hard into his seat. After they left ground, it was a steep climb for a few minutes. Then the plane reached the right altitude, leveled off, and the noise from the propellers faded. Thereafter, the flight from Dallas to New York City, the first airplane ride he had ever taken in his life, was surprisingly smooth.

From the pre-Kennedy Idlewild Airport, Mike took a bus into the city, where he found himself almost overwhelmed: the noise, the traffic, the enormous buildings looming overhead, the steady flow of people rushing who-knows-where through midtown Manhattan—this was much different from the small Texas town where he had lived, and he didn't like it at all. He got off the bus at the Port Authority bus station, then followed signs to the correct counter, where he finally bought the right ticket.

With that in hand he went upstairs three floors to the correct gate and clambered aboard a bus. It was almost full and he had to go all the way to the back before he found a seat. As he walked he couldn't help but notice perhaps a dozen other young men who looked a lot like him, and it wasn't hard for him to guess that they were all headed to the same place.

As Mike sat down, the guy next to the window stuck out his hand.

"Hi, I'm Mike Brennan from Wisconsin, and I'm going to West Point. How about you?"

That brought a smile to Mike's lips, and he felt relief at breaking the ice with a kindred spirit. Neither of them had ever traveled far from home, and just making their way alone through New York City had been one of the most challenging and exciting things they had ever done.

"Mike Mewhinney, from Denton, Texas, and yes, I'm going to West Point too."

They were soon sharing their giddy anticipation of the next day, when they would formally become Cadets. Both were a little bit concerned about the tough discipline they expected to face at West Point, but they readily trivialized it, for they were two colts on the loose, ready to lope through the wooded highlands above the Hudson River in upstate New York. Both boys— and they were still that—were brimming over with excitement about soon becoming Cadets, a coming-of-age experience both had long dreamed of and were now about to actually taste. They had no way to know it then, but these two would become the closest of friends at the academy.

The bus got to West Point in the early afternoon and the would-be Cadets checked into the Hotel Thayer, where they were billeted in a big room filled with forty or fifty cots. There they left their nearly empty suitcases and were told that, on their last day as civilians, they had the freedom to walk around West Point.

They had to report in officially on the following morning, so the two Mikes decided to walk around and check out the "campus." The Hotel Thayer was just inside the gate from the small town of Highland Falls, and they walked directly north a full mile along Thayer Road in the cool shade of tall hardwood trees. It was a quiet day and a pleasant walk, with large stone houses uphill on their left and the magnificent Hudson River far below them on their right. Then they came to the academy itself, which seemed like nothing more than a castle that had been brought here from somewhere in medieval Europe.

First they passed the Cadet hospital on their left that rose four or five floors, then other massive gray stone buildings towered above them on both sides of the road. They didn't yet know exactly what these buildings were, but clearly they were at the very heart of West Point.

Some car traffic was moving both ways, other civilians were walking around, and now and then even a few Cadets went by wearing tight gray coats with high black collars and white pants. The two Mikes agreed that they looked very good indeed—even a bit dashing. This, after all, was what they had long aspired to be, and on the edge of admission they were eager to belong. As one Cadet walked past them, Brennan tried to ask a perhaps meaningless question.

"Excuse me, sir, I just got here for . . ."

But the Cadet ignored him and kept walking, so Brennan turned to Mewhinney.

"That was sort of rude, don't you think? Not what you'd expect from a Cadet."

"I think he must know who we are and I guess he just doesn't want talk to us yet. They say we're going to have to go through some Mickey Mouse plebe stuff for a while, and they probably don't want to make friends with us just yet. I guess that will come later in the summer."

They kept walking and suddenly found themselves beyond the buildings, and off to their left front was an enormous expanse of neatly trimmed grass. Beyond the buildings they had passed on their left, more gray stone buildings stretched away from them and lined one side of the grass, all partially masked by tall elms. A few hundred yards away, these buildings intersected with another row, which was arrayed parallel with the road along which they walked.

But that side of the Plain, too, was somewhat obscured by tall, formal-looking trees, their massive branches seeming to somehow grace the cold gray stone. Everything they had seen of the academy so far, Mewhinney had to admit to himself, was nothing less than breathtakingly beautiful. Then Brennan's loud whisper interrupted his reverie.

"Wow! This must be the famous Plain we've heard so much about, right?"

"Yeah, I guess so. But you could put a whole bunch of my high school football fields out there and never run out of room. And look, those rows of stone buildings seem to come together back there, so behind that screen of trees it looks like there are buildings on two sides of the Plain."

"Yeah, and look up above them on that hill. Is that a church?"

"I think it's called the Cadet Chapel. But it looks more like some old French cathedral than any chapel I've ever seen."

They continued walking north along the east edge of the Plain, and some distance ahead it looked like they would enter a thin forest of trees. But the road they were walking along also swept sharply to their left some distance ahead, thus outlining the two open sides of the roughly rectangular Plain.

As they watched, a small red convertible with its top down could be seen following the curve in the road and heading toward them. Even from a distance, they both knew it was one of those fancy new Chevrolet Corvettes. And as it got closer, they also could see that the driver was a beautiful blonde woman wearing sunglasses.

The car slowed as it drew near them, then passed and stopped no more than twenty or thirty yards beyond them. Both were speechless as they turned and watched, but before they could even say anything, a Cadet came running out of one of those gray buildings, then opened the passenger door and hopped in. They were close enough that they could see the couple turn and smile at each other, then she stepped on the gas and they were gone. Brennan could barely speak.

"Did you see that?"

"Did I ever! Let me tell you, that really confirms it for me, I sure did come to college at the right place!"

As for myself, I had wanted to become a Cadet for as far back as I could remember. My father was a fighter pilot in World War II and he had stayed in the Air Force after the war, reaching the rank of colonel before I went off to West Point. And while my father was not himself a West Point graduate, he worked with some men who were, and they were sometimes at our house for a dinner party or some such social gathering.

On most of those occasions, I was just a kid and not really part of their company, so I only overheard them from the hall. But as I listened to their stories, whether of their days at West Point or of flying or of fighting in the Second World War, I thought they were glamorous.

We moved every two or three years, so when I was a senior in high school, I had lived a lot of places and met a lot of people, but really had no home base other than wherever my father was currently assigned. That meant I was the "new kid in town" every few years and my senior year in high school was living in Virginia outside of Washington DC. I knew I had virtually no chance of winning an appointment from my local congressman, so hoping for a break, I applied for a "presidential" appointment to West Point, a small number of which are reserved for the sons of career military. And while my grades and other activities were good enough that I was found "qualified" by West Point standards, my credentials weren't really competitive with those of other applicants and I missed out.

But I wasn't ready to give up just yet. The previous year, a neighborhood friend whose father was a naval officer had faced similar frustrations. So he took a week off from school, walked the halls of Congress, and simply asked for an appointment in the offices of every member. To everyone's surprise, that won him an appointment to Annapolis. Seeing such success, I did the same thing. And sure enough, at almost the last minute, I won an appointment to West Point. And the most important thing I learned was that unless you ask, you just never know . . .

On the first day of July 1962, I took the train to New York City, then caught the bus up Route 9W to West Point. I was anxious, of course—scared would be a better word—and didn't sleep well that night in the Hotel Thayer. I was up by dawn and after a hurried breakfast, went outside, where olive drab army buses picked us up in groups. We had been told to show up at the army gym between 8:00 and 10:00 a.m., and we knew, from stories we had all heard, that a harsh welcome awaited us. Only a few went on the early buses, therefore, while the rest of us sort of dragged our heels.

But what were we afraid of? Sure, we expected a certain amount of harassment and even picky behavior from the juniors and seniors who would be there to guide us through the next two months of summer. So they'll yell at us, maybe make us run around a bit. But I had been yelled at and made to run around before—some of my high school coaches could be just hell on wheels! So how bad could it be to be harassed by Cadets, our secret heroes, rather than coaches?

There was general agreement among us that the first few days might be tough, but once we had our own handsome Cadet uniforms and could walk around West Point in them, dazzling the girls up from New York City, why, it wouldn't be that bad at all. We knew that Cadets couldn't touch us, so what could they possibly do that had made West Point graduates describe Beast Barracks as being so terribly hard?

No, we all agreed, we had been yelled at and punished by parents and teachers and coaches, we had even slept on the ground as Boy Scouts. This might be a little bit tougher for a while, but it would just be more of the same. No big deal.

Finally, around 9:00 a.m., the pressure got to be too much and I just hopped on a bus.

But I, as well as all the other innocent aspirants who had spent the night in the Hotel Thayer, simply had no idea what awaited us.

No idea.

High Aspirations

3

Beast

At the army gym, Deme Clainos stood in a long line of other future Cadets. There were administrative steps to go through before actually beginning Beast Barracks, but no big deal. He had already gone through a freshman year at the University of California in Berkeley, one of the best schools in the country, and he was not intimidated at all by the prospect of a harsh reception at West Point. A somewhat typical California guy, Deme was laid-back and cool and not worried at all about a supposedly difficult Plebe year. He was very bright, and no matter what, a devilish grin seemed to radiate from his face all the time.

Deme's father had graduated from West Point in the late thirties, and as his assignments changed, Deme's family had moved every two or three years. This gave him more real-world experience than his peers, including the three years he had lived in Germany. During his first year at Berkeley, Deme decided, just as his father had, that he wanted to go to West Point. While his father did not discourage him, he left it all up to Deme to find his way there. But that made him want it all the more, and after he won the appointment of a California congressman, Deme had gotten on a plane east with the blessings of both his parents.

The ticket punching in the army gym was not too complicated, and once again he heard stories from other young men, just as he had in the hotel the night before, about how tough

Beast Barracks would be. But most of these other guys had just gotten out of high school, and relative to them, he was sort of a man of the world. No matter how tough it might be, he knew he could get through the petty harassment with ease.

Along with all the rest, after his name was matched in their paperwork, someone tied a six-inch stiff paper list with about ten printed lines on it to his belt. Then, still carrying his suitcase, he was sent back outside to find yet another line. He wasn't there long, for as part of a group of ten, he was led by a soldier in a khaki uniform out onto a sidewalk that went diagonally across the edge of the Plain. Deme looked around, and the view over the Plain was spectacular. West Point really was quite beautiful, he thought, but they were moving toward a mass of stone buildings, behind which, as he would soon learn, was Central Area.

Before the use of gunpowder, strife was almost constant across much of Europe. To protect themselves, their family, kin, and serfs from such dangers, local regents built castles protected by massive stone walls. When threatened, the serfs left their lands, picked up pikes or bows and arrows, and fled behind these walls for protection.

Most mass movement into a castle was through a main gate, but there were always smaller openings in the castle walls, which became known as "sallyports," through which troops might sally forth to attack besieging forces. That is why the massive West Point Cadet barracks, modeled on castles, are perforated by portals known as sallyports some twenty feet wide and nearly as tall, crowned with an arch that supports the wall above it.

From its earliest days, the architects who built the stone buildings at West Point were careful to re-create elements of European castles from many centuries in the past. That meant massive gray granite buildings with rigid right angles and topped by crenelated battlements. But it also meant that the main access into the two major areas of Cadet barracks, Central Area and North Area, was through sallyports.

During the late fifties, Deme and his new classmates had all seen a big hit movie about West Point, *The Long Gray Line*, starring megastars Tyrone Power and Maureen O'Hara. From that, if nothing else, they all knew that, on a fall Saturday morning during football season, there was really nothing quite so thrilling as watching thousands of Cadets in spotless gray uniform coats over white pants, wearing plumed hats and shining brass accoutrements and carrying gleaming rifles on their shoulders, come pouring out of those sallyports and onto the Plain.

But that would come later. For now, Deme realized that they were moving toward such a sallyport. And as they got closer, he heard noise building, noise that had started as faint buzzing. But as they drew nearer, the noise soon grew into an absolute roar. It was men yelling, lots of them, and he had never in his life heard anything like it.

As they entered the sallyport itself, the roar became overwhelming and almost deafening. They came back out into the sun inside Central Area, and it seemed like a movie mob scene, men running madly in all directions. Then Deme was startled by a Cadet yelling at him personally.

"YOU MAN IN THE BLUE SHIRT! DRIVE OVER HERE!" He was startled and his mouth dropped open. The words came from an angry-looking Cadet in a white shirt, white hat, white gloves, and gray pants. And he was looking right at Clainos. Deme had heard about and expected some version of a "drop that bag!" drill, but had not expected the thunderous wall of noise. He walked a few feet toward the Cadet and stopped.

"STAND AT ATTENTION, MISTER! BACK STRAIGHT, ARMS AT YOUR SIDES, HEELS TOGETHER! LOOK STRAIGHT TO YOUR FRONT AND NOWHERE ELSE!"

Deme tried to comply, but the noise was overwhelming.

"NOW DROP THAT BAG!"

He released it as fast as he could, but, as he had been warned, it was not fast enough.

"TOO SLOW! PICK IT UP!"

They went through several repetitions of this, along with corrections to Deme's posture. The Cadet's voice modulated, but not his manner.

"I didn't tell you to bend over! Keep your arms straight and your eyes to the front! You are a New Cadet and that is your title! When you speak to me or to any other upperclassman you will start with 'Sir'! What is your name?"

"Sir, I'm New Ca . . ."

"I CAN'T HEAR YOU!"

"SIR, I AM NEW CADET CLAINOS!"

The Cadet grabbed the list on Deme's belt and read his name, then suddenly his voice lowered in volume again, still loud but no longer yelling.

"Mister Clainos, I am going to teach you the proper New Cadet position of attention. First of all, keep your back straight and pull your chin back into your neck and make some wrinkles."

It was a strain, but he could do it okay, he guessed. But he was wrong. And the Cadet in front of him was suddenly shouting again.

"I SAID TO GET YOUR NECK IN, WHACKHEAD! NOW DO IT!"

Deme strained as hard as he could, but it wasn't good enough.

"PULL IT BACK, MISTER! I WANT TO SEE SOME WRINKLES!"

Clainos was utterly terrified and was suddenly worried about what he was doing. But after a bit more yelling, the Cadet's voice volume lowered once again.

"Okay, Mr. Clainos, you are now bracing. At all times until June Week next year, whenever you are in the Area of Barracks, unless you are in your room, you will maintain this position of attention, including bracing. Do you understand?"

His chin and neck were starting to hurt and he could barely burble out a response as he turned to look at his oppressor.

"Sir, I don't think you . . ."

The Cadet exploded.

"EYES STRAIGHT TO THE FRONT, SMACK! NO MORE GAZING AROUND!"

Clainos froze as his tormentor softened his tone once again.

"Whenever you answer me or any other upperclassman, you have three possible answers: 'Yes, sir,' 'No, sir,' and 'No excuse, sir'! Do you understand that?"

Clainos snapped his eyes back to the front, unsure of what this man-turned-into-beast might do to him but also careful that his answer comply.

"Yes, sir."

This demon in white shirt and hat leaned close, flames licking Clainos's cheek as he screamed.

"I CAN'T HEAR YOU!"

"YES, SIR!"

His voice grew soft again.

"Mister Clainos, look across the Area directly to your front and you will see a half flight of steps leading up to a landing and a door. On that landing you will see a man in a red sash. Do you see him?"

"Yes, sir!"

"All right, he is the Cadet first sergeant for the Third New Cadet Company, to which you have been assigned. Now you double-time over there and report to him. Move out!"

Bob Lowry had been one of the first to report that morning. A tall, lean blond from New Mexico, he had played tennis in high school and had carried the tuba in the band. He did very well academically, but his real dream had long been to go to West Point.

To that end, he spent a year at the New Mexico Military Institute. While he had been anxious, at the last minute the appointment from his congressman finally came through, so he headed east, eager to wear Cadet gray. He was a bit anxious about the harsh treatment he had been warned to expect, although quiet reflection convinced him that it couldn't be that bad. Growing more eager on the plane, he expected to just sail through Plebe year. But within the first few hours of Beast, he was in as much of a whirl that day as anyone else.

After reporting to the Man in the Red Sash, he was assigned to a bare room containing three beds, three chairs, three metal lockers, and three desks. He met his two roommates, but only briefly, for the yelling from upperclassmen was continuous. And these New Cadets not only had to brace all the time, but they also had to run everywhere they went.

During the next seven hours, he would get his hair cut unbelievably short, pick up a mattress, pillow, sheets, and blanket, be measured and tested and receive shots at the hospital, be fitted for and receive olive drab fatigues, black combat boots, black shoes, black socks, white underwear, gray pants, and a short-sleeved white shirt. After visiting each station, every new Cadet would report back to his "Man in the Red Sash"—his new Cadet company Cadet first sergeant, who was in charge of administrative details—where the cardboard sheet tied to his belt would be checked off and he would be sent to another station.

Upon their arrival at West Point, new Cadets entered the Fourth Class, and freshmen there are called Fourth Classmen. Similarly, sophomores are Third Classmen, juniors Second Classmen, and seniors First Classmen. The more common terms used, however, are Plebes, Yearlings, Cows, and Firsties, though Plebes could only use the numerical class designation.

The New Cadet companies all started Beast Barracks with about 130 new Cadets and about thirty-five upperclassmen—half Firsties and half Cows. These New Cadet companies were further broken down into roughly thirty-man platoons and seven-man squads. Every New Cadet would become intimately familiar with his Second Class squad leader, for that man was his personal interface with West Point: the man who would teach him how to wear his uniform, how to spit-shine shoes, how to shine brass, and how to keep his room and meager possessions (all army issue) in strict conformity with Regulations U S C C. And if they were lucky, he would also give New Cadets tips on how to succeed.

But there was no personal friendship involved, for New Cadets were always standing in a position of attention, uncomfortably bracing, and they opened their comments to all upperclassmen with "Sir" and addressed them as "Mister" surname. After having been to a few stations, the Man in the Red Sash told Mr. Lowry to report to a squad leader standing in the middle of Central Area with a handful of other New Cadets. Soon after Lowry joined the group, they were given rudimentary instruction in basic marching, which was not terribly difficult. But it was important, because at 5:00 p.m. (or "1700 hours" in military parlance), the entire class would march out to Trophy Point—no more than a quarter-mile away—where they would be sworn in as West Point Cadets.

The details began to blur for all New Cadets, but around noon they somehow ended up inside the cavernous mess hall for the midday meal known to Cadets as "dinner," to distinguish it from the evening meal, known as "supper." Ten-man tables were filled with seven or eight New Cadets and two or three upperclassmen, where they stood behind chairs and waited. The New Cadets, of course, were all bracing and sweating and the upperclassmen all seemed to be yelling at them. After ten minutes or so, all 808 New Cadets in the class of 1966 and perhaps 200 upperclassmen had found their places, and the order was given to "Take Seats!"

Once all were seated, New Cadets were given fine-tuning directions: they were to brace at all times, to sit on the forward four inches of their chair seats, and to keep their eyes on the plate in front of them. Then they were told that, after serving themselves from the circulating plates of food, they were to take bites no bigger than half the size of their little fingernail. They were to put the bite into their mouths and return their hands to their laps before chewing.

If their bite was too big, or they began to chew too early, they would be told by one of the upperclassmen on their table to "sit up!" That meant they were to put down their fork, sit at attention with back straight and arms at sides, then do as they were told. They would soon learn that this would be the moment for them to recite certain information they would either be required to memorize, like Schofield's lengthy definition of discipline, or the movies playing in the army theater (to the screening of which they, of course, would have no access) and their male and female actors, or the number of days remaining before a number of special dates, like certain football games, certain holidays, and, of course, graduation.

On the first day, however, the only information that could be asked of them was biographical, which instantly became the subject of ridicule by the upperclassmen. So they sat there silently, staring down at their plate full of food and wishing they could eat some of it. No, they wished they could eat *any* of it!

When the meal ended, all new Cadets stood up, the food on their plates having barely been touched, and returned to their company barracks in Central Area. These were buildings four stories high that had been built before the Civil War, and while a tourist might have thought they looked like some sort of romantic castle, to New Cadets they were more like medieval dungeons. Their stone walls were solid, with the original cast iron staircases, but they had been upgraded at some time in the early twentieth century with radiators heating each room. Empty fireplaces from more than a century ago were still there, but their rifles were stacked in front of them and, like the rest of their room, were kept spotlessly clean by the New Cadets living there.

The afternoon was filled with more administrative running around from station to station, always controlled by the Man in the Red Sash checking off the list attached to their belts. In line at the barber shop, Mewhinney was stunned by the suddenly bald-looking New Cadets, his classmates, coming out. He had never worn his hair so short, and when he was finally sitting down in the chair, he asked the barber to take it easy on him. The barber's response was a smile and the electric shears. But that was only a mild surprise next to the jolting ferocity with which he and his peers were treated by members of the upperclass cadre.

One very important, though intangible, piece of instruction that first day was also given to every New Cadet by his squad leader, and that was their introduction to the Cadet Honor Code, by which they were all bound from that very first day: A Cadet will not lie, cheat, or steal, or tolerate those who do. This code was administered by a Cadet Honor Board, which would hear all charges of dishonorable conduct by Cadets and decide guilt or innocence by vote, without any intrusion into their affairs by officers or faculty.

If the board found a Cadet guilty, the academy's administration would support the board by dismissing the guilty party from the academy that very day. The underlying belief that supported this summary action was that no man whose dishonor was proven should be allowed to sully the honor of any other Cadets, even by his simple presence in their midst.

The tradition went back to the middle of the nineteenth century, though it was never written down as a formal honor code until just after World War II. Rather, it was simply understood by all Cadets that a man's word was his bond, and breaking it was grounds for dismissal.

However, despite this common understanding about a man's word of honor being above challenge, for a long time both before and after the Civil War, the common attitude of Cadets was basically that the West Point experience pitted all of them against the staff and faculty. If a faculty member caught a Cadet cheating, then under academy rules he would be severely punished, though usually not expelled. But Cadets at the time saw their relationship with staff and faculty as adversarial, and anything they might do to stay afloat academically, short of telling a lie, was considered acceptable. Cheating in class, to them, did not bear the same gravitas as breaking the word of an officer and a gentleman, and it was not considered an honor offense.

By the early twentieth century, however, Cadets began to

realize that cheating was a form of deception and so was seen by them as dishonorable. The first Honor Committee, which formally reviewed all alleged honor offenses, was established by Superintendent Douglas MacArthur in 1922. But the actual Honor Code itself—"A Cadet will not lie, cheat, or steal"—was not written down until 1947 under Superintendent Maxwell Taylor. While toleration had also been considered an honor offense, those words—"or tolerate those who do"—were not formally added to the Code until 1970.

Finally, the New Cadets were all clothed in their newly issued underwear, socks, white shirt, gray pants, black belts and shoes. They formed up by company inside Central Area, then began the march out to Trophy Point for their swearing-in ceremony. Suddenly seeing crowds of cheering civilians lining the sidewalks as they marched past, mostly parents and families of New Cadets who had stayed around for this, was like seeing people from a different world.

For Mewhinney, whose family had stayed behind in Dallas, the whole march-out and swearing-in was really a blur. The sun was hot on his face, his back was wet with sweat, and he rigidly stared straight to his front, terrified that some upperclassman would start yelling at him again. He raised his hand with the rest and repeated the words as they came, but after a truly hellacious day, he was beginning to have real second thoughts.

Mike was still a bit confused about that Cadet with the blonde babe in the Corvette he and Brennan had seen only the day before, and he still hoped that all the harassment he had endured so far would soon diminish. But given what he had heard from his squad leader and other upperclassmen so far, that was a painfully fading hope.

After the ceremony, they were somehow all back in the mess hall again. More yelling, more New Cadet feelings of insecurity, more wondering what they had gotten themselves into. And more hunger: two or three tiny bites of meat, three or four of green beans, a glass of milk, and that was about it. Then they were moving out into the dark, getting yelled at yet again as they tried to remember where their rooms were.

But back from supper was no time for rest—indeed, they sometimes thought there would simply be no rest, for the never-satisfied upperclassmen seemed like so many fire-breathing hellions. And once back in their newly assigned rooms, the upperclassmen assigned to be their squad leaders were always with them, showing them such basic things as how to fold their uniforms in lockers, how to spit-shine shoes, how to polish brass, how to disassemble and clean their M-1 rifles. Their civilian clothes were placed in their small suitcases and locked in a trunk room somewhere, and they would not see them again until the following June. It was all army issue now, and so disappeared their only physical reminders of the civilian life they had left behind.

This instruction by squad leaders, with more elaboration as they were issued more clothing and gear, would go on for the next nine weeks, but with constant harassment. There was never enough time to do what was required of them, and though they were initially eager to learn, it wasn't long before they felt like they were being forced to drink from a fire hose. On that first night they had so much to do in preparing their equipment for the morrow that, when "Taps" was blown at 2300 hours, virtually none of them were ready to go to bed.

But they did, because that was what they were ordered to do. And when the lights went out on that first night, many of them began having second thoughts: they may have been warned that it would be tough, but it was not at all what they had expected—in retrospect, how could it have been? Before falling asleep, many asked themselves what on earth they had gotten into.

As days passed, new Cadets were issued more uniforms and accoutrements. They were required to learn more information from *Bugle Notes*, a book they had been issued that seemed almost silly ("What is the definition of leather?" "How many lights in Cullum Hall?" "How many gallons in Lusk Reservoir?"). But New Cadets had been required to learn these factoids for a very long time, and the institutional attitude seemed to be that if it was good enough for us, then it's good enough for this next cyclical set of New Cadets.

West Point cares a great deal about how its Cadets look, particularly in parades or otherwise in the public eye. Consequently, all Cadet uniforms are tailor made, usually with several fittings required, and those started on our very first day.

Over the first week we would be fitted for and receive our various uniforms. First were our parade uniforms: woolen Full Dress Gray coats, which were uncomfortably high-collared and studded with forty-four brass buttons on their chest and swallowtails; black parade hats known as "tarbuckets"; a half-dozen starched white crossbelts and the brass buckles that held them together; and heavily starched white duck pants.

Next came the slightly less formal woolen Dress Gray coats, also high-collared, black-trimmed, and uncomfortable, along with heavy gray woolen pants with a black stripe down the side. After that was our class uniform of charcoal woolen shirts and black ties; our summer uniforms of long-sleeved and short-sleeved tan khaki shirts and pants; for athletics, personalized (name printed above academy crest on left breast) West Point T-shirts and gray gym shorts worn with black sneakers; for winter formal wear, one heavy woolen long overcoat that reached to mid-calf and had a cape over the shoulders; for class, one heavy woolen short overcoat that reached to mid-thigh and had no cape; for rain, a gray raincoat with cape; for off-duty wear, a light gray cotton zippered jacket; for showers, a light cotton bathrobe, shower slippers, a bar of soap, and several white towels. With the addition of a gray scarf, black gloves, and both gray and white hats, these were our uniforms. They all had names, and for the following four years, except when home on leave, these were the only clothes we would wear.

By the end of the second week, we had been fitted for and received most of this tailored clothing and had then folded it in our lockers or hung it on wall hooks. Once we started feeling comfortable that our uniforms were all squared away, we unexpectedly began a traditional Beast delight known as "Clothing Formations."

After supper, we would have an hour or so to shine shoes, polish brass, write a quick letter home (required), and arrange our rooms for inspection. We would then all be ordered down into Central Area wearing fatigues and boots, where we would form up by companies.

After some yelling at latecomers, the senior Cadet captain in Beast Barracks—known as the "King of Beasts"—would shout out some uniform:

"Full dress gray under arms."

That meant black shoes, full dress coat, white pants, tarbucket hat, starched white cotton crossbelts with brass buckles, and carrying our M-1 rifles. We were told we had five minutes to reappear in that uniform and stand in formation, then would be dismissed and race back to our rooms.

Once we were dressed, the crossbelts were difficult to put on to complete our uniform, and roommates had to help each other. Even so, five minutes was enough for most New Cadets to make it back into formation. But there were stragglers, and the yelling started. After a head count showed we were all there, a new uniform was shouted out:

"Uniform sierra!"

Once again, we raced back to our rooms and scrambled to get into the new uniform. But this time, we had only three minutes.

When the time expired, a smaller number of our class was in ranks, and now the yelling within the barracks by upperclassmen at New Cadets echoed out into the Area. And another cycle began.

"As for class under raincoats with black sneakers and tarbuckets!"

That mix of uniforms, as with many others to follow, made no sense at all but only added to the turmoil. And that was the point. This was the first time-and-distance performance pressure put on the whole class together, and some of us would do better than others.

After five or six cycles of this, we were all exhausted and our rooms looked like tornadoes had blown through them, with items of clothing belonging to their three New Cadet residents scattered everywhere. And after our last clothing formation came "Shower Formation."

Inside these nineteenth-century barracks buildings, toilet and shower facilities were all in the basement, or, in Cadet language, "the sinks." A few minutes after the last clothing formation, we were ordered to report to the sinks in our bathrobes and slippers, carrying a bar of soap and a towel. We were then lined up against the wall, and the upperclass cadre for each company ordered New Cadets to brace until they had sweated through their flimsy bathrobe material.

That may sound strange, but it's what we did. Some people sweated faster than others, but it took everyone at least ten minutes, during which time the cadre walked up and down the line finding fault in all those scumbucket New Cadets and yelling like thunder.

Once we began to sweat, individuals were singled out and placed in one of a long line of shower stalls, where the yelling continued:

"Hot water on! Cold water on! Wash! Wash!"

With or without the noise, a hot shower provided some relief. But then the next order came, and it was literally a shocker:

"Hot water off, cold water on! Rinse, you whackheads, rinse!"

We all stupidly obeyed, even though in the shower stalls we were out of sight of our upperclass tormentors, and the cold water was truly a shock, chilling us to the bone. After these shower ordeals, we returned to our rooms and had perhaps half an hour before "Lights out!," which was strictly enforced.

Every night, that routine became our Beast Barracks goodnight kiss from the King of Beasts, and we dreaded it. But we also endured it, as so many who had come before us also had.

Some New Cadets were luckier than others in roommates assigned. Well into Beast, Mike Mewhinney was still trying to figure out when he would get the blonde babe in the Corvette convertible. But one of his roommates was an absolute misfit who should never have even showed up, and we will call him Mister Goofball.

At first, Mike and his other roommate tried to help Goofball with his uniform, his shoes, everything. But he just couldn't seem to learn. He was so inept that he barely ate a bite at meals, and his name quickly became legend. Whenever they had some free time and were working on some aspect of their uniforms in their rooms, their squad leader usually came down to give them tips and pointers. But even then, Goofball would screw up and anger the one guy who was trying to help him survive.

Although Mike and the other roommate were at first impatient with Goofball, they soon realized that whenever an upperclassman inspected them, either in ranks or in their rooms, Goofball immediately became the target of their rage. Consequently, he only lasted through the last week of Beast. But before then, Mike was delighted to have him there, because he was the shit-magnet of the company, which caused upperclassmen to more or less ignore everyone else, and especially Goofball's roommates. So when he left at the end of Beast, and although they didn't get along well personally at all, Mike was really sad to see Mister Goofball leave.

New Cadets also received intensive training in marching and other soldierly skills, to include everything from physically draining calisthenics, to correctly erecting a pup tent, to producing the blood-thirsty roars required of them as they strained through exhausting bayonet drill. And although they marched to three meals each day, and there was plenty of food available, they simply were not allowed to eat more than a very small amount.

All New Cadets would lose weight during their first, trying year, especially during those first nine weeks of Beast Barracks. But because weight loss had been such a problem in the past, in the summer of 1962 academy authorities required that, each night after supper, every New Cadet would receive one piece of fresh fruit and one small carton of milk in their rooms. But this hardly changed the system, for it made the upperclassmen even more stringent on what they let New Cadets eat at regular meals. Our unofficial class slogan, cobbled together by Beast cadre, was "With fruit and milk we'll get our kicks, for we're the boys of sixty-six."

For the first four weeks of Beast, we New Cadets had virtually no "free time." Although our schedules allowed us a few open hours on Saturday and Sunday afternoons, we were not allowed to leave the Area of Barracks, where we might meet parents or other visitors who might have brought food, or actually buy real food at the Hotel Thayer. Rather, such moments were precious to us as we tried to play "catch-up" on shoe-shining and brass-polishing and other minutiae that were suddenly of crucial importance. And we were desperate for food of any sort, just to stave off the starvation we all felt looming large.

By the end of the third week, Art Mosley thought he was ready to quit. In addition to the constant running and harassment, he had begun to feel physically weak. Already a slender man, he had really angered the First Classman who sat at the end of his table over something trivial about the use of Avogadro's number, which Art knew well and the Firsty did not.

And as he was challenged intellectually by other upperclassmen, it only got worse, because he was smarter than they were and he just couldn't keep his mouth shut. The result was that, for countless days, though his plate was always filled, Art was allowed to eat nothing at all. His only source of nourishment for several days was the fruit and milk each evening, and he was surprised to learn that the apple core went down just as easily as the rest, with not a trace of it left. When asked condescendingly after a few weeks if he was hungry, he even told his squad leader several times that he thought he was literally starving. But that brought only sneers and derision.

For Art, the pressure was becoming just too much, and he wondered if he could still transfer to Harvard, which had already admitted him out of high school. At least there, he thought, he would be able to eat and sleep and act like a normal human being instead of being treated like some dog—or worse, because at least dogs were fed.

One midday after three weeks and another empty dinner, he went back to his room and, alone for once, decided to eat his entire tube of Crest toothpaste. The taste was familiar, and he found some satisfaction in it. But after the tube was about half empty, he felt nauseous. Then he felt himself involuntarily gagging as his body tried to vomit. But with an empty stomach, all he got were dry heaves.

The noise echoed down the hall, and soon his squad leader was at his door.

"What's the matter, Mister Mosley? Are you sick?"

Art's face had blanched.

"No, sir, I just . . ."

The near-empty toothpaste tube was on the floor in front of him, and his squad leader instantly knew what had happened.

"Oh, so you're a toothpaste bandit, are you, Mosley? I don't think we've had one in this company yet."

But instead of helping him, the squad leader mockingly laughed as he shouted the news down the hall to other upperclassmen. The news spread like wildfire, and the next thing he knew, Art was being subjected to loud ridicule everywhere he went.

"Well, look, here comes Mister Sparkle! How was the toothpaste, Smackhead?"

"Face it, Mosley, you're a weakling and you're just not tough enough to make it!"

"Why don't you just quit now and go home to Mommy, she'll take good care of you!"

Art's hunger endured, but this public mocking about his supposed weakness just went over the top. He might not be a star Plebe, but he would never give in to those jerks. By God, they would not drive him out, and he would never quit! Too bad for Harvard, because I'm not going there, I'm staying here!

After weeks of heavy pressure, hard work, and what felt like near starvation, New Cadets felt themselves fitting in with other young men who had quickly become their classmates, closest friends, and key allies. And they knew how to march and look good on parade. When they heard the shouted order "Squads Left!" or "Squads Right!" they knew the sequence of steps to take and their timing so as to attain the desired result.

When done by West Point Cadets, squad drill made the whole formation, from a distance, look like it initially dissolved and then, as if by magic, reformed, but only after having changed its direction of march by ninety degrees. It was a most impressive sight for a tourist, but difficult-to-absolute-hell for a New Cadet to learn.

By the end of Beast Barracks, this latest cohort of New Cadets was truly drained. But, according to tradition, that was the way it was supposed to be. The old saw they had all heard soon after they arrived was that, in 1962, West Point stood for "160 years of tradition untouched by progress." And the upperclassmen who taught new Cadets the ways of West Point seemed perfectly satisfied with that perception: This is going to be hard, they seemed to say, harder than you ever thought possible. And before you make it, we will make sure that we first grind you down to nothing as Plebes and then, over the ensuing three years, allow you to build yourselves up into real men.

But you won't all make it, because many of you are too soft and too lazy. So when we discover weaklings among you, we will do our best to run them out. And if we are unable to complete our work in weeding you out, when the Corps returns for Reorganization Week right before Labor Day, you will be outnumbered and other upperclassmen will finish the job for us.

That was a dread all New Cadets harbored as Beast Barracks

ended. The class of 1966 had started with 808 New Cadets, and while none of them were allowed to quit during the first four weeks of Beast Barracks, during the second four weeks they began to leave in flurries. Many more would leave during Plebe year, and only 579 would graduate four years later.

4

Plebes at Last

There were at the time twenty-four Cadet companies, each made up of roughly one hundred Cadets who lived together in a specific area of the barracks. Because of the need to divide class schedules, half of these companies were designated as the First Regiment (A-1 through M-1), the other half Second Regiment (A-2 through M-2). Actual behavior of Cadets in the two regiments, despite rumors to the contrary, was virtually indistinguishable.

Each of the twenty-four companies operated as units for parades, inspections, intramural competition, marching to meals and chapel—and yes, in those days, chapel attendance on Sunday was mandatory. Attendance was routinely taken, and skipping chapel—or any other mandatory formation, such as class or meals—would mean a very harsh punishment.

As Beast drew to a close, the cadre warned New Cadets to expect genuine ferocity from the mass of upperclassmen who would return for Reorganization Week. Those were unsettling warnings, and whatever awaited us, which was still unknown, it was clear that our assignments to our regular companies would not be fun.

But actually, when Mike Brennan joined his regular Cadet company, he found that most returning upperclassmen had much more to do than to waste time hazing this latest set of former New Cadets, who had been transformed, by getting through

Beast Barracks without quitting, into Plebes. There were count-less new duties for Plebes, including delivering copies of the *New York Times* to every Cadet in his room before breakfast (the only source of news for Cadets as there were no television sets avail-able, and radios at the time—forbidden to Plebes—provided only music); mail delivery (the only mail Cadets cared about came from girlfriends, and even if you got a letter every day—few did—it was never enough); and minute calling/shouting in the hallways before every meal and other formation ("SIR, THERE ARE FIVE MINUTES BEFORE FORMATION FOR PARADE. THE UNIFORM IS FULL DRESS GRAY UNDER ARMS. FIVE MINUTES, SIR!").

Such duties were harassment enough. But the much greater concern for Plebes soon became the heavy academic load they all had to shoulder.

When the military academy was established in 1802, it was the only engineering school in the country, and, indeed, it led that field until well into the latter part of the nineteenth cen-tury. That academic orientation endured, and when classes began after Labor Day in 1962, all Plebes had the same class schedule, and it was set in stone: they would all become engineers, and no electives were available for the first two years. After that, only one elective was available during the second semester of Second Class year, and one each semester of First Class year.

Unless a Cadet was granted credit for a given course he had taken at a civilian college before arriving at West Point, all were stuck with a math-and-science-heavy curriculum that had var-ied little over preceding decades. For the first two years, all were required to take ninety-minute classes in calculus and associ-ated mathematics six days a week (yes, Saturday morning classes were obligatory). In addition, the schedule during those first two years included English, a foreign language, astronomy and astronautics, graphics and measurements, physics, chemistry, psychology, American and European history, comparative lit-erature, and military heritage. And also during those first two years, on three days each week, every Cadet spent ninety minutes in the army gym where they were taught and tested (and had to earn a passing grade) in swimming, gymnastics, wrestling, and boxing.

During their Second and First Class years, Cadets would study electrical engineering, atomic and nuclear physics, fluid and solid mechanics, propulsion, ballistics, world history, international relations, civil engineering, leadership, constitutional and military law, and (a class taught in no other college) history of the military art. And physical education in the latter two years only occurred once or twice each week and was oriented more toward enduring sports that might be pursued by graduates as officers: racquetball, tennis, squash, and golf.

This was a draining academic schedule. And there was more, for after classes, athletic competition was required of all. Unless Cadets competed seasonally in one of twenty-odd intercollegiate sports or a similar number of club sports (about one-third of Cadets did), then intramural athletics were mandatory, ranging from football and soccer through wrestling and skiing to lacrosse and tennis. Competition was between companies, and winning one's own regimental championship, let alone the brigade championship, was a very big deal.

But that was not all. Formal parade and inspection in ranks precluded intramurals on Tuesday (First Regiment) or Thursday (Second Regiment) afternoons. And after Saturday morning classes, the entire Corps of Cadets was subject to room and personal inspections. That meant forming up in Full Dress Gray uniforms with starched white crossbelts, shined brass buckles, tarbucket hats, and spotless shoes and rifles so that each company tactical officer could closely examine the Cadets under his care for flaws.

After inspection, the entire Corps of Cadets would parade on the Plain before tactical officers, tourists, or anyone else who felt like watching. And while such a formal display of carefully rehearsed and beautifully clothed Cadets marching close order drill may have been impressive to onlookers, for Cadets it was a major pain. But it was also just the way it was, so we simply endured it as best we could.

The rest of Cadet life, of course, was far from easy, and there was little way to physically escape it. The only departures from West Point for Cadets came when football games were played in New York City, of which there might be one or two each fall, and the annual Army-Navy game in Philadelphia. And even these meant only, after the game, being released for one evening in the big city, with mandatory formation at the train or bus station at midnight that same Saturday. Other than those trips, overnight trips might be arranged for club sports like rugby, judo, or rifle, or for other condoned extracurricular organizations like the Rocket Club, the Debate Council, or the French Club. But Cadets normally were allowed to be absent from West Point only for the relevant Saturday night.

Deme Clainos spied such an opportunity early in the fall, and that was membership in the Cadet Math Forum. Because of his one year at Berkeley, where he was a math major, he had tested out of the first year of calculus to which the rest of us were subjected. And his special expertise in that field allowed him to join the Math Forum, most of whose other members were upperclassmen.

So in early October, he and the rest of the Math Forum got on a bus to Poughkeepsie, New York, where they would spend the night in a hotel. For all Cadets, finding a legitimate justification for getting off post was good enough in and of itself. But the purpose of the trip, and its real attraction, was for the Cadets to meet math majors at Vassar College.

On this trip, Deme did not want to flex his math muscles at all. No, he just wanted to meet some pretty girls. And he didn't care if they knew anything about math at all, other than one and one make two.

There were about thirty members of the Math Forum, all eager to meet members of the fairer sex. But, to their great dismay, only about a dozen math-happy Vassar girls showed up. Sitting in a bar later with a handful of other Cadets, Deme tried to put the best face on it: however empty of pretty girls, this evening they could legally drink alcohol in a real bar, and that sure beat staying in the barracks back at West Point.

But as they talked together, Deme realized that he had a lot in common with one of the other Forum members, a Cow named Clair Thurston. Clair was surprised to hear that Deme had studied math at Berkeley, and he was full of questions about comparative teaching methods. This was stuff that Deme could rattle off with no hesitation at all, and he did. Very quickly, other Cadets got bored and flaked off, leaving Clair and Deme delighting in their discussion about math at one end of the bar.

It didn't take long before they realized that, not only were they both army brats whose fathers had been career officers, but that they had gone to the same American high school on a U.S. base in Heidelberg, Germany. Their stays in Germany had overlapped by one year, but Clair was one year ahead of Deme, so they never took any classes together. But they had mutual friends among other students and they had had the same teachers. Best of all, they laughed together over remembered high school high jinks, in particular some of the crazy things other students had done but who had narrowly avoided arrest by U.S. military police in a foreign country.

So it was that Deme and Clair became fast friends, and they stayed such for the next two years, until Clair graduated. But before that, he gave Deme some tips and even helped him get on other legitimate trips that would let him get away from West Point for trips to New York City.

Other than such official trips, however, Plebes were not allowed to leave post at all, even over normal Cadet Christmas leave. As upperclassmen, there was a bit more tolerance on weekend leaves, for which Cadets were released after Saturday parade and had to return before supper the next day, Sunday. Yearlings were granted one weekend each semester, Cows two, and Firsties got to take five weekends anytime they chose throughout the calendar year.

Holy cow! With that kind of freedom, Firsties were living large!

As we slugged it out in class, sports, and parades, upperclass Cadets were literally counting days until Christmas vacation—or rather, Plebes were counting days for them, another humiliating bit of "Plebe Knowledge" for which we were responsible at all times whenever so asked by any upperclass Cadet. And if you didn't know, there would be hell to pay: what are we having at the next meal, how many days until the football/basketball/baseball game against X University, how many days until Christmas leave, spring leave, and graduation, and what is the movie showing at the army theater, including the names of the male and female leads—this even though it was not possible for anyone but Firsties to attend such movies, and then only under strained circumstances.

So every night, Plebes found some refuge in being in their rooms, either studying, writing letters, or shining shoes and brass. Normally, all Cadets are required to be in their rooms from "Call to Quarters" after supper at 7:00 p.m. until Taps at 11:00 p.m. During that time, certain Cadets—usually Cows—would have the added duty each week of checking the Cadet rooms within his subdivision—usually eight to sixteen rooms—by stopping outside each Cadet room door and simply asking "All right?" The normal response to that query came from one of the Cadets inside the room and was usually simply another "All right!" But that response meant that all Cadets assigned to that room were either inside it or, if absent, their absences were authorized under the Regulations of the United States Corps of Cadets.

These inspections took place twice each evening, and at times that were randomly changed, so that you never really knew when the subdivision inspector, or "subdiver," would be coming around. And this "All right" response was a matter of honor. That is, if you lied and said "All right" when one of your roommates might have, in violation of regulations, slipped out to meet a girl (which happened all too infrequently in our Rockbound Highland Home), then the man who had answered "All right" would have, by that act, committed an honor offense. And that was a very serious matter that, if found to have occurred by the Cadet Honor Board, would result in the miscreant's dismissal from the academy.

These Regs were kept in a light blue binder inside every Cadet room. Authorized evening absences were quite limited, such as being in the library, in the gym, or in the hospital. We were not authorized to be visiting a friend in his room, and if you got caught (which was commonplace), you would be notified the next morning that the tactical officer (normally a captain or major assigned to discipline and otherwise manage the hundred-odd hormone-leaking young men in each company) had received a report on your absence from your room. Having been so accused, the Cadet who got caught had to submit a written explanation to the Tac.

If the explanation was something as innocuous as playing monopoly in a classmate's room, the normal punishment would be administered: five demerits and two punishment tours. A Cadet was allowed twenty demerits each month, and demerits were awarded for such sins as falling asleep in a lecture, being late to class, or being found to have dust in your rifle barrel or poorly shined shoes at the inspections preceding our two weekly parades.

These assessments of dusty rifle barrel or of a marginally less than mirror-like shine gleaming from the toes of carefully spit-shined shoes, of course, were all somewhat subjective. The same was true for room inspections Saturday morning before parade, when one's bed might be found to be less than perfectly made or underwear to be less than precisely square as arranged in each Cadet's locker.

That meant you didn't want to be on the bad-boy list of the inspecting officer. And because you lived in close quarters, an angry Firsty could be very hard on any underclassmen who had done no more than irritate him on some minor issue.

The day-to-day life of a Cadet, in other words, was quite difficult and trying, and within a short time after their arrival, most Cadets simply loathed the place. But you acquired that attitude during Plebe Year, when the sledding was really tough. It seemed then that the upperclassmen were trying to make you acknowledge to yourself that West Point was just too tough and so make you quit. But those who really wanted to earn a West Point diploma, like Art Mosley and countless others, had become quite stubborn: no upperclassman was going to drive them out, and, come hell or high water, they weren't going to quit!

As new Plebes, of course, we were little different from those who had preceded us over the previous century and a half. Our October was interrupted by the Cuban Missile Crisis when, on October 22, President Kennedy announced in a televised news conference that Russian missiles were being deployed in Cuba. He added that the United States demanded their removal, and that the U.S. Navy would blockade that island until Russia agreed to remove them.

As mentioned earlier, we did not have access to television sets and our only source of news was the *New York Times*. Largely insulated from the regular army as we were, there was never any threat to us personally. Within a few weeks, the problems were negotiated away and political concerns over World War III with the Soviet Union were largely dissolved.

We lost the Army-Navy game during our Plebe year by a forgotten but humiliating score, for Navy had a new quarterback who was more skilled than any other player any of us had ever seen play football before: Roger Staubach, who would win a Heisman Trophy and later star for the Dallas Cowboys, even winning Super Bowls. Needless to say, even though he was only a sophomore—or "Youngster" in Annapolis parlance—Army was no match for him that day.

That loss cast a certain gloom over the Corps, and life for

Plebes was made no easier. But that game was the last in the football season, and West Point's true "Gloom Period" began to set in: gray uniforms, gray walls, gray skies, gray faces, and that icicle wind pouring down the Hudson Valley, sweeping over the snow-covered Plain, and slashing into every Plebe's frail sense of self-worth—will this trial never end? But then, as the weeks before Christmas narrowed down to days, the upperclassmen, unusually mirthful as they got ready to leave for their homes, tended to leave Plebes alone.

5

Holiday Cheer

Then they were gone, and only the Plebes and the normal tactical officer cadre were left at West Point. Suddenly, we could walk through the Area without bracing, could shout and halloo to classmates inside the cavernous mess hall named after George Washington, could even go to see a movie in the army theater, so long as we were back in our rooms before Taps. It was a fresh and heady feeling. But we were not allowed to drink alcohol, let alone to possess any in our rooms. And for us, going off post was strictly forbidden.

If upperclassmen had still been around, of course, it would have been stupid if not impossible for Plebes to try to hide alcohol in any of our rooms. Virtually all of our possessions—the only exception was that we could have one six-by-four-inch framed photograph on the back of the top shelf in our locker—were government-issued Cadet gear, and there was nowhere to hide anything else in our bare rooms, which were theoretically always subject to inspection. But with no upperclassmen inside the barracks, that became no real threat at all.

Acquiring such illicit alcohol, however, was another thing altogether. The legal drinking age in New York at the time was eighteen, so technically that was no barrier. But when it came to an eighteen-year-old Plebe having the guts to disguise himself in forbidden civilian clothes, then brazenly walk off post to buy alcohol and bring it back to thirsty classmates—aye, there's the rub, laddie.

For one thing, we had no civilian clothing, and it would be virtually suicidal to go off post into Highland Falls wearing our uniforms. That was because the regular army officers who made up the staff and faculty at West Point were almost all academy graduates themselves, and they knew every trick we might try to pull, for not so long ago they had lived through the same experiences themselves. They all actually lived on post with their families, and if they were to see us in Highland Falls, where they often shopped, the naked sleeves on our dress gray uniform coats or overcoats practically screamed "Plebes!"— whom they knew were forbidden to go off post. Checkmate.

But with enough nerve, maybe not. In an effort to treat First Classmen a bit more like adults, the academy had long allowed them to keep civilian clothes inside their lockers in their rooms. But those First Classmen were, by this time, far away on holiday leave and would not return, we knew, until they had to on January 3, 1963. At the time, Cadet rooms simply had no locks, which meant that we had full access to whatever civilian clothes we might find inside Firsty lockers, hopefully some that even came close to fitting us. So one afternoon a few days before Christmas, Art Mosley and I decided to dress up in Firsty civilian clothing and head into town.

Our plan was to buy four cases of beer in a liquor store and conceal them inside what were known as B-4 bags—canvas suitcases with voluminous pockets on each side, secured with heavy zippers, that we had all been issued. We decided that, to conceal and carry into the barracks four cases of beer, we would need three B-4 bags and at least three classmates to carry them.

I had met our classmate Deme Clainos in an English class, and he was very much of a free-spirit risk-taker, like Mosley and me. And as soon as I mentioned the plan to him, he was eager to play. So on the cold, wind-swept day before Christmas, with deep snow covering the Plain, the three of us put on the civvies of absent Firsties, then tucked our B-4 backs under our arms and nonchalantly walked the mile to the gate into Highland Falls. From there, we brazenly strode out into the normal civilian world.

We found a liquor store within a few hundred yards, and the best deal we could get was four cases of Ballantine Ale in short bottles for less than ten dollars. We paid our money, then unpacked their cardboard cases and carefully stowed the bottles out of sight inside the B-4 bags. But we certainly couldn't lug them back to the barracks, so we had to take a taxi.

At the time, West Point and Highland Falls were serviced by the Bosch Taxi Company, a local family-run company with a small fleet of older vehicles. These had a wide bench seat in the rear and two more fold-down seats between it and the front bench seat. That meant you could theoretically seat as many as eight passengers, and the Bosch Taxi people were in the habit of picking up as many fares as possible for each run on or off post.

When we got back out on the street with our bulky B-4 bags, within minutes we were able to flag down an empty Bosch taxi. The three of us, with our B-4 bags in our laps, filled the back bench seat entirely, and when we closed the door, we could barely suppress our glee. All we had to do now was get back to Grant Hall, little more than a mile away, then into Central Area, where we would quickly disappear with the beer. But as the driver turned and headed back toward the gate into West Point, a woman on the sidewalk flagged him down.

That made us all a bit uneasy, and I said so to Mosley.

"Relax," he said, "it's just some woman. She doesn't care what we're doing, she's just looking for a ride back on post, that's all."

But as the driver stopped, the woman opened the front door and herded a six-year-old boy into the front seat in front of her, then turned and spoke to someone we couldn't see, who had been hidden by a sign. Then the person she had spoken to, obviously her husband, stepped forward and opened the back door into our compartment, and we saw that he was wearing the uniform overcoat and hat of an army major. He helped a ten-year-old girl into the cab, then reached in and flipped down the two small fold-down seats.

Mose and Clainos and I all pulled our feet in as close as we could and hugged our B-4 bags tight to our bodies. Then the major, whose ring on his finger told us he was a grad, put his daughter into one of the fold-downs and gave us a silent ugly look. It was a tight fit; he wedged himself into the other flip-down seat, then closed the door behind himself.

The three of us on the rear bench seat shrank to the size of mice—no, fleas. Dear God, how did this happen? We had gotten all the way to the store, bought the beer, and were on our way back with our spoils in high spirits when this looming menace had climbed into our cab with us.

As the taxi moved forward, fantastical thoughts flashed through our minds. Maybe he doesn't know, we thought. Maybe he thinks we're not Cadets, we're just soldiers, that's all. But as the taxi moved through the slushy street, the bottles of beer began to hit each other.

Clink. Clink-clink. Clink.

We held our breath on the back seat bench and prayed for deliverance. We were waved through the open gate, then picked up speed. And again, the glass bottles began to sing.

Clink. Clink. Clink-clink-clink-clink. Clink. Clink-clink. Clink.

The three of us were mortified, and we were sure that we were about to get written up and spend the rest of Christmas vacation eating a raft of demerits and walking eternal punishment tours in Central Area. The wife in the front seat turned and whispered something to her husband that we couldn't hear, and he nodded to her but kept his eyes straight to the front.

And then once again the musical bells erupted merrily:

Clink. Clink-clink-clink-clink. Cl-cl-cl-clink. Clink. Clink-clink.

Then we were at Grant Hall, the obvious drop-off spot for Cadets, and the driver stopped. The major opened the door and got out as Mose and I struggled to get our B-4 bags out past him. He had a grim look on his face, but he stood aside as we hoisted our B-4 bags out, clinking with every move. The major's daughter had opened the other door and Deme Clainos had gotten out, dragging his steadily singing B-4 bag behind him. Then he put it down on the street and pulled out his wallet. We owed the driver two dollars and fifty cents, and Deme only had two dollars. I reached in my civilian pocket and pulled out two quarters, but now the grim major had suddenly turned into Santa Claus. He grabbed my arm.

"Never mind, mister, I'll pay the driver when we get home."

I was flustered: he had called me "mister," so he obviously knew we were Cadets. And there could be little doubt for him about the source of the clinking.

"Tha-thank you, sir . . . I mean, we've got the money . . ."

He held up his hand to stop me.

"Don't worry about it. Matter of fact, I did something similar once myself, so have a Merry Christmas."

His wife's cheery voice rang out:

"Merry Christmas, boys!"

As we clinked our way into the barracks in Central Area, a wave of relief washed over us. Man, that had been close! But even at West Point, it seemed that holiday cheer was everywhere, even for lowly Plebes like us! So Merry Christmas, indeed!

6

Christmas Dinner

On Christmas Day, eight men in our class whose names had been randomly selected were invited to be guests for Christmas dinner in the superintendent's house. So it was that Mike Brennan, the son of a milkman in rural Wisconsin, found himself wearing his forty-eight-brass-button full dress coat when he approached the most impressive, and oldest, building on post.

Built in 1820, the superintendent's house, more formally known as Quarters 100, was a museum piece of Early Americana. Built in the Federal style, it is a large three-story brick house painted solid white with black roof, shutters, and portico and four tall chimneys rising from the fireplaces below that were once its sole source of heat. An imposing presence, it stood solemnly alone with the somewhat smaller but similarly styled and colored commandant's house next to it, both overlooking the Plain from its western side. Mike and the seven other Plebes invited to Christmas dinner went up a few steps onto the porch, where winking holiday lights with red and green festoons of Christmas decorations hung from the front door and porch roof.

One of them pushed the button, and a cluster of bells attached to the front door jingled sweetly when it was opened. A uniformed butler smoothly escorted them into a thickly carpeted living room filled with overstuffed chairs, heavy brocade drapes, large gold-framed paintings of unknown military figures from the past, and gleaming tables and lights. And on the far side of the room was the superintendent, Maj. Gen. William C. Westmoreland, and his wife, Katherine. She was formally attired in a full-skirted red silk dress with pearl necklace and earrings, while Westmoreland himself was decked out in a gleaming blue uniform with stars and gold braid on his sleeves and medals practically dripping from his chest.

Mike lost his breath for a moment. Wow. He had never seen anything like that back in Wisconsin. Wow.

Westmoreland was a rising star in the army who had commanded the 187th Airborne Regimental Combat Team when it made two combat parachute jumps during the Korean War. In the eyes of Cadets then, as well as those of everyone in the army or the civilian world who knew of him, he was red hot, a shooting star in uniform.

After the butler introduced them by name, stiff handshakes were followed by the Cadets hesitantly sipping from the non-alcoholic hot cider they had been handed. Then there was a bit of small talk initiated by Mrs. Westmoreland.

"Gentlemen, the general and I want you all to feel welcome in our home for Christmas dinner. I'm not in the army myself, of course, so please feel as comfortable with me as you can. My name is Katherine, as you know, but my friends all call me Kitsy, a name which I hope you gentlemen will use as well when you address me."

For the entire evening, not one Plebe called her "Kitsy," but rather stayed formal with "Mrs. Westmoreland"—as they knew, without warning, they should. But Kitsy did try to make them relax and asked some open-ended questions of them all, to which the Plebes anxiously mumbled their expected responses: yes, ma'am, they had all enjoyed the mandatory chapel service they had attended that morning; no, ma'am, the cold was not bothering them; yes, ma'am, they had all spoken on the pay phone with their parents; no, ma'am, they had never been inside such a large old house formally decked out in holiday cheer quite like this one.

Soon enough, they went into the dining room and saw name tags on the far side of each plate. When all had found their places, they stood stiffly, then sat down at Westmoreland's bidding. The white tablecloth was elaborately stitched with white embroidery that, eventually, they realized was different sizes of the academy crest as well as crossed rifles, sabers, and cannon that denoted various branches of the profession they had chosen to pursue. The plates were the finest china with hand-painted academy crests and whose outer edges seemed to be actually encrusted with gold. Mike was a bit intimidated by the number of forks, knives, and spoons that were on both sides of each plate as well as beside the small plates and bowls that seemed to hover around the main one. But Kitsy had anticipated this, and she was smooth.

"Gentlemen, I want you all to feel right at home for Christmas dinner with the general and myself. We welcome you into our home and hope that you will find a small escape from the rigors of Plebe year as our guests. Now, you will see quite a bit of fine cutlery that is part of each place setting in front of you."

The Plebes all smiled but said nothing.

"Don't worry, these are just the formal place settings that come with the position of superintendent, but you may as well learn about such social customs now, for some day, several of you may very well rise to general officer's rank, and we don't want you to be unprepared."

Uncomfortable nodding and smiles, but not a word came out of a Plebe mouth as uniformed servants began placing plates of salad in front of each Cadet. Kitsy went on.

"Now, the first rule you should try to remember is that, as different courses are served, you should use the knife or fork that is farthest away from your plate. For instance, as salad is now being served, you should use the small fork and knife that are farthest away from each side of your plate. Do you see what I mean?"

Kitsy picked these utensils up and began cutting her salad

with them, then put a small forkful into her mouth. The Plebes followed suit, but they all took tiny bites, then put down their utensils and put their hands in their laps before chewing. At least they didn't have to brace, though they felt like they should have. All, however, kept their eyes on their plates while they chewed. Ah, the enduring habits of being forced to eat meals as a Plebe.

The main course was Christmas turkey, with stuffing, cranberry sauce, mashed potatoes, gravy, the whole works. They were just getting into this when they heard the doorbell ring. A moment later, the butler entered the room, went to Westmoreland's side, and whispered something to him. At that, Westmoreland stood up, asked his wife to be excused, and followed the butler out into the hall. The Plebes tried to ignore this interruption, but in the middle of Christmas dinner, who could that be?

A moment later, Westmoreland reappeared and addressed the table.

"Is there a Mister Brennan here?"

The blood drained from Mike's face as he stood up.

"Yes, sir, that's me."

"Okay, Mister Brennan, come with me."

Mike was terrified, his legs suddenly numb as he walked. What could this possibly be that had called him out of a formal Christmas dinner in the superintendent's house? His first thoughts were ones of panic about his family—had something bad happened?

Then they were at the front door, where Mike saw his roommate, Billy DuPhus, standing just inside. DuPhus was having a hard time with Plebe year, and he had several times told Mike that he it was just too much for him, and he was trying to build up his courage enough to quit. Mike had tried to talk him out of it, though DuPhus was, to say the least, a bad fit who just couldn't seem to do anything right, and he would finally quit a month after Christmas. But now, here he was at the Supe's house, wanting to see Mike. What could this possibly be? Before Mike could say a word, Westmoreland took over.

"Okay, Mister DuPhus, here is Mister Brennan. But before you say anything to each other, the more I think about it, I believe this is an issue important enough for your other classmates to hear as well. So if you don't mind, I think we should go into the dining room, so follow me."

As they strode the few steps, Mike's personal fear began to recede. But what could this possibly be about, for DuPhus to interrupt Christmas dinner at the Supe's house? When they got to the end of the table, Westmoreland spoke.

"Okay, Mister DuPhus, please tell my wife and your classmates what you told me."

"Well, sir, back in Beast Barracks, my squad leader told us that if we ever had a really hard problem during Plebe year, the first person we should ask for help would be our roommate. And sir, Mister Brennan is my roommate, and I have that kind of problem."

"All right, Mister DuPhus, tell us all what that problem is."

"Well, sir, I've been dating a girl from New York City, she's been coming up to see me nearly every weekend. And I don't know if I'm in love with her or not. But yesterday, I got a letter from her, and she tells me that there's another boy she's been seeing, and she thinks she loves him and she wants to break it off with me. So I just don't know what to do, and that's what I want to ask Mister Brennan."

"That's fine, Mister DuPhus, I think I understand completely. You got the proverbial 'Dear John' letter from your girlfriend in New York City and you don't know what to do. Is that correct?"

"Yes, sir."

"Okay, but before Mister Brennan says anything, I've lived a bit longer than you men, so let me give you my considered advice. Now, I was a Plebe here myself thirty years ago, and I think I know what you're facing."

Westmoreland paused and faced the table. Mike had never

seen anything like all the gold and color he wore, and in all that finery, he looked like something out of a movie.

"The most important thing you must all remember is that, since that first day you arrived here, when you were sworn in at Trophy Point, you have all become members of the United States Corps of Cadets. And the authorities at West Point have long known that this first year at West Point, your Plebe year, is both the most trying and the most important. In order for you to be able to focus on what you must do and learn, then, all your civilian possessions have been taken away and replaced, so that whatever you have now is all Cadet issue. As for a girlfriend during Plebe year, she can only be a distraction from more important things, and you just don't need one. That means you can just forget about the one who wrote you that letter. So remember, if the army thought you needed a girlfriend, they would have issued you one. Do I make myself clear?"

The stunned Cadets around the table mumbled a response. "Yes, sir."

"All right, Mister DuPhus, enough of this about 'Dear John' letters. Trust me, you'll get over her. Now, have you been to the mess hall for Christmas dinner yet?

"No, sir."

"All right, as long as you're here, let's make a place for you and you can join our feast."

Mike grimaced. So DuPhus, who would quit West Point less than a month later, had just managed to get his Christmas dinner in the home of the superintendent.

But DuPhus and his finagling to get Christmas dinner at the Supe's house were less important than what Mike had just heard Westmoreland say, and he still refused to believe him. Girlfriends are a distraction during Plebe year? And if you needed one, the army would issue you one? What kind of crazy talk is that?

Only six months ago he had left Helen, his high school sweetheart who was literally a farmer's daughter, back in Wisconsin. They wrote to each other every day, and truly, the stars had aligned for them. He knew that he loved her and she loved him as no couple had ever loved before, and they were destined to be together forever. He dared not say that, however, so when Westmoreland asked if they understood, he had meekly assented.

But life is long, and he would show them.

7

World Politics

Since we had no television and were not allowed to go off post, our social activities were limited. Families or girlfriends could visit and stay in the Hotel Thayer, but most of us were far from home and had little hope of either.

That meant that, in addition to going to the movies every night over the Christmas holidays and playing handball or basketball with classmates when we could, we read the papers a lot. And in various parts of the world, it seemed that wars were being fought pretty much all the time. In Cameroon, in Indonesia, in the Congo, in Iraq, in Algeria, soldiers on both sides, whether supporting rebels or defending governments, were dying every day. And even then, the United States had contingents of troops deployed in more countries than we could possibly have known. Therefore, it was not terribly unusual when, on December 29, we read in the *New York Times* that 11,000 American soldiers were stationed in far-off mysterious South Vietnam, where they were supposedly helping suppress a Communist rebellion. And of that number, more than 100 had been killed or wounded during the previous year.

At the time, Communism, to us, meant pure evil. Vietnam had been a French colony from back in the previous century, but when Germany defeated and occupied France in 1940, its ally, Japan, took control of the French colonies in Southeast Asia, including Vietnam. Then in 1945, when the defeated Japanese left, a local Vietnamese rebel force known as the Viet Minh took control of the country. They had fought against their Japanese occupiers with some U.S. aid, and they asked to be recognized as an independent country. Their leader, Ho Chi Minh, asked for American support, stating that they had fought to overthrow rule by a European empire just as the United States had won independence from England in the late eighteenth century.

But Americans were most afraid of the specter of Communism, which ruled the peoples of China and Russia, and which we were afraid was spreading like the plague. Because Communist states ruled by fiat and allowed no vote to private citizens, Communism was seen as antithetical to the American way of life.

In 1949 Communist forces under Mao Zedong had defeated the Chinese Nationalist Army under Chiang Kai-shek and took control of the land mass of China. The Nationalist Army retreated to the offshore island of Taiwan, which is smaller than Massachusetts, where they maintained the pretense of being the legitimate government of China. But the reality was that Mao established the People's Republic of China and ruled that nation with the Chinese Communist Party, a rule that was still going strong during the 1960s.

Korea had also been divided in half after World War II, with Russian Communists propping up the government in the North and Americans supporting the South. The Korean War started in 1950, when North Korean forces washed over most of the peninsula. Then an American army under Gen. Douglas MacArthur landed at Inchon on Korea's western coast—one of MacArthur's true strokes of genius—and drove the North Koreans all the way north to the Yalu River, the border between Korea and China. But Mao didn't like that, so in 1951 waves of Chinese forces crossed the Yalu into Korea and drove the Americans back to the Thirty-Eighth Parallel. There, stalemate fighting endured until an armistice was signed in 1953. So American soldiers had fought against the Chinese Army in Korea, and China was clearly considered an enemy state.

Thereafter, a serious question that haunted American politicians asked who was responsible for the fall of China. To Americans in the early 1960s, Communist rule anywhere in the world was anathema. And if we had to spend blood and treasure to stop the seeming wave of Communism in the world, we would do so.

Under President Truman, therefore, after World War II, American ships, planes, military supplies, and money allowed the French to return to Vietnam and reassert themselves. That meant the Viet Minh, widely supported by the Vietnamese people, who wanted an end to colonial rule, had to go underground to continue their fight against the French. Thereafter, the People's Republic of China as well as Stalin's Soviet Union began sending supplies to Ho Chi Minh's forces, and, riding a tidal wave of popular support, the Viet Minh began to win their war against the French.

In 1952 Eisenhower was elected president of the United States, with a heavy charge to end the Korean War. This he effectively did with an armistice signed by both sides in July 1953. But the French were pleading for more U.S. assistance in their war against the Viet Minh.

If granted, we would oppose the growth of Communism in Vietnam, and such opposition was considered by most Americans to be good. But in so doing, we would also support French imperial rule in one of their colonies, which would mean suppressing the aspirations of Vietnamese people wanting freedom from under that colonial yoke, which was bad. That meant a very tough call for our political leaders.

So Eisenhower did follow Truman's lead and sent the French weapons, vehicles, radios, and some light bombers, all left over from World War II. But he steadfastly refused to send ground troops under any circumstances. According to Robert Donovan in *Eisenhower: The Inside Story*, he said, "No one could be more bitterly opposed to ever getting the United States involved in a hot war in that region than I am. . . . I could not conceive of a greater tragedy for America than to get heavily involved in Vietnam."

To Cadets in 1962 and 1963, Vietnam was still some never-never land in the mysterious Orient on the other side of the world. So to us, stories about civil unrest or rebellion against the French and their heirs in government were of little, if any, significance.

Within a few months, though, more noise from South Vietnam came our way. On May 9, 1963, we read in the *New York Times* that on the previous day, May 8, South Vietnamese Army troops, under orders from their Catholic rulers, had opened fire on 20,000 Buddhists who were demonstrating in a parade in Hue, killing a dozen of them. This was seen as quite dangerous to peace and stability in the region because the population of South Vietnam was about 70 percent Buddhist and only 10 percent Catholic.

For the most part, over the preceding century, the Vietnamese Catholics had been recruited to their religion by the French, and their conversions can fairly be seen as those of rice-bowl-Christians. That is, once they were co-religionists, these Vietnamese converts became the loyal satraps of the French, for whom they ran the sometimes-oppressive government of their fellow Vietnamese people. And after the French had left Vietnam in the middle 1950s, these Vietnamese Catholics had stayed on in political power. Not surprisingly, frequent clashes continued between the Buddhist masses and the Catholic elite and their families. But never before had these politico-religious struggles been quite so bloody.

The president of South Vietnam then, Ngo Dinh Diem, was of course a Catholic, as were all the top members of his government and senior military commanders. After the bad press he got in America for this shooting, he announced he would change the ways in which Buddhists were treated by police and soldiers. In fact, he did nothing, and routine oppression continued.

But this or any other world news was noted by us little more than in passing, for we were finally getting to the end of Plebe year. As graduation during the first week in June grew closer, we knew that our stored-up angst would soon explode in a river of delirious delight. That was the focus of our attention, and some political nonsense from somewhere on the far side of the world was not very interesting at all. Despite our disinterest in Vietnam at the time, however, that attitude would slowly but surely change.

Then June Week and the graduation of the First Class arrived, and the routine hazing, harassment, and humiliation that Plebes had endured for a year came to an end. Graduation Parade on the Plain took place the day before actual graduation, after which the Plebes in a given company would line up and, for the first time in a year, act like normal young men. That is, they could look around, talk to each other, and were no longer required to brace.

After Graduation Parade, the Plebes in a given company would stand side by side in their company area, and all the upperclassmen in that company would slowly go down the line and shake the hand of each Plebe. That handshake was the formal sign of "recognition," after which there was no more "Mister" that prefaced one's surname. Rather, these former Plebes could, for the first time, address all other Cadets by their first names and expect them to reciprocate. That may sound like nothing, but it was central to former Plebes being treated by other Cadets as, and their feeling like, real human beings rather than the lowest form of life. After this momentous set of handshakes, we rejoiced that we were no longer Plebes, and naturally enough, we thought it was "all over."

It was not all over, of course, but we wouldn't become aware of that for several more months, when we returned to the academic year as Yearlings. Even so, after giving us an arduous, difficult, and trying Plebe year, the class of 1963 had finally graduated. Then the class of 1966, Plebe year over, was released for thirty days' leave.

While we were home on leave that June, there was little in the news that really interested us, probably because we ignored everything that didn't involve drinking beer or chasing girls. There was one photograph, however, that no American could ignore, and it truly stunned us all. This picture was an unexpected outcome of the riots in Vietnam the previous May in which South Vietnamese troops had killed quite a few Buddhists.

A number of Buddhist monks in Vietnam decided to make an unanticipated, and, to Westerners, somewhat mind-blowing demonstration to the world of their dissatisfaction with the ways Buddhists were being treated by the Catholic leadership of their country. On June 11, 1963, several hundred monks, their shaved heads, saffron robes, and sandals clearly identifying them, marched into a main traffic intersection in Saigon, then the capital of the Republic of Vietnam, or, as it was more commonly referred to, simply South Vietnam. They formed an open square, in the center of which one of them, Thich Quang Duc, sat down in a lotus position. Then another monk poured a five-gallon can of gasoline over him, after which the would-be martyr ignited himself and turned into a blazing pyre.

A photograph of the monk's erect seated figure with flames billowing out to one side in the wind was on the front page of newspapers around the world. President Kennedy was horrified, and he openly demanded that Diem change his government's treatment of Buddhists. Once again, the promises came, but on the ground in Vietnam, nothing changed. But to us at the time, while it was a gruesome picture, we really didn't understand the underlying politics, which we continued largely to ignore.

8

SPNSS, 0025 Hours, 21 November 1965

Mike Brennan couldn't even feel his feet as they flew, his eyes locked on the Marine who came out of the guardhouse and waited for the slowly approaching vehicle. With his back turned to us, the guard held out his hand and the station wagon came to a full stop. The driver was Helen, Mike Brennan's fiancée, and she rolled down her window and seemed to be talking to the guard, though we were still too far away to hear her voice.

Miraculously, Helen was still talking as we reached the circle of light surrounding the main gate area. Then, as we huddled by the goat cage, the guard post door opened and a second Marine guard stepped out into the cold. With that, the passenger's door of the station wagon opened and Juliana stepped out and walked a few steps toward the front of the car, clearly at the edge of tears as she started talking to the second Marine. Now we could hear their voices, and Juliana sounded distressed— good girl! But by this time our attention was focused on the padlock that held the gate closed.

Inside the pen, beyond the shed, we saw our target—a big white goat with enormous horns painted bright blue and gold, Navy's colors. And the horns were much bigger than anticipated, three or four feet long and sweeping back and out to either side. Brennan's throat was suddenly very dry.

Mewhinney quickly slipped the tip of the small crowbar through the hasp of the lock, bracing the tip against a metal post. Then Clainos wrapped a black towel intended to silence noise around the lock, squeezed it tight and nodded his head. None of us yet knew if this would do the job, but on signal, the other four of us pulled the end of the crowbar down hard.

The lock broke with a loud snap and we all froze, thinking the Marines must have heard it. But a glance showed both still talking to those poor girls, who, according to plan, said they were looking for the Naval Academy and must have taken a wrong turn on that cold, lonely night. They were both very sad but seemed suddenly thrilled by those handsome Marines. Both girls were in "high flirt," their tears shifting seamlessly back and forth with soft laughter.

Two beautiful girls looking for help on a freezing Saturday night in November—those poor Marines never had a chance.

Clainos removed the broken padlock from the gate and pushed it open. Then Deme Clainos and Mike Brennan stepped into the cage, each carrying a previously prepared length of rope with a loop and a slipknot on one end. Mike started slowly walking around the right side of the hut, his rope loop held open in one hand while Deme started around the other. As they moved, they remembered Captain Slinky's words, that the goat might well attack them, but now that they saw the goat's huge horns, it was far from an idle threat.

Their breathing was shallow, their arms and legs stiff as they slowly approached that big white animal, shaking his huge—no, enormous!—blue and gold horns. Then a new voice from around the guardhouse had all five of us flat on our faces, trying to ignore the cold, wet mixture of mud and goat shit in which we were all suddenly lying face down.

9

Buckner

In early July, we returned to West Point and were bused out to Camp Buckner. That was to be the setting for the first "real army" field training for our class, and we were eager for it.

Camp Buckner is a spray of barracks buildings, mess halls, and various other administrative structures that hover on one edge of Lake Popolopen, surrounded by some 17,000 acres of forested hills that made up the West Point military reservation. That meant no civilians were allowed to enter this area, a vast array of rocky and heavily wooded terrain that was used solely for the field training of Cadets.

By the time we arrived back at West Point that July, more than a hundred of the 808 young men sworn in as Cadets in the class of 1966 were gone. A few failed academically and a few others were dismissed because of their amply displayed sheer ineptitude for military service. But most who left did so of their own accord, having decided, at some point during the Plebe year grind, that life, shall we say, had other doors for them to open. That meant we had a hard core of just under seven hundred men left in our class who reported to Camp Buckner as new Yearlings.

We were broken down into five companies of roughly a hundred and forty men, each of which was further broken down into twenty-man platoons. A somewhat artificial competition was structured between companies, based on grades we got from parades and inspections. But most of us rather ignored that aspect, for this would be our true launching as real soldiers as well as, in off-duty hours, our "sort of" summer camp at the beach. We expected to learn a lot about the army, of course. But we also expected to have a lot of fun on the ranges and in the field while doing such things as driving tanks, adjusting artillery, and firing rifles and machine guns.

Each Buckner Cadet company was assigned to sleep in a set of barracks, which were long, one-story aluminum buildings containing rows of steel-frame bunk beds with sinks, showers, urinals, and commodes at one end. Each of us also had a wooden footlocker, as well as hooks on the wall, where all our clothing and army gear was kept. In other words, the buildings in which we slept looked just like regular army barracks of the era.

Every platoon of twenty-odd Yearlings was commanded by a new First Classman, who slept in another barracks building but commanded us in formations during the day. He was responsible generally for our overall adherence to regulations, supposedly just like things worked in the real army. In the spring of our Plebe year, upperclassmen in our companies had all told us we had a lot to look forward to at Buckner, and many of them said it was the best summer of their lives. The command structure there was not enforced with the rigidity of Plebe year, of course, and we played the game, reporting and saluting while still calling Firsties "sir."

We would spend nine weeks at Buckner, during which we were never allowed to leave the cantonment area. Even so, on weekends we were off duty and could even invite girls to join us. We had parades on our own parade ground at the far end of the lake, and we wore starched white uniforms for these. But after parade we were off duty until supper Sunday evening, and West Point had done its best to see that our idle hours were not empty or boring.

Saturday nights, there were dances in Barth Hall, which was perched on the edge of Popolopen, another aluminum building, but almost square in dimensions, with the upper half of the walls made up of screens that gave access to the moonlight, the faint breeze, and the weird cry of the loons from somewhere down the lake—all in all, a very romantic setting. If we did not have girlfriends from back home coming to join us, there was always a bevy of blind dates available through the Cadet Hostess, Mrs. Holland. She only needed about twenty-four hours' notice, so if you wanted a date for Saturday night, you had to sign up before supper on Friday.

You never knew what you'd get on such a blind date, which is why we referred to the system as "the Holland Tunnel"— some of the girls were truly gorgeous, others less so. But whatever you got, she was also willing to take a chance on just "some Cadet," and hormones were spilling over on both sides. Cadets had to wear their formal starched white uniforms to the dances, and these were seen as handsome by most girls who had volunteered to step into the dark in accepting a blind date at Buckner. And the starched stiffness of the pants, as well as the rigidity of the high-collared brass-buttoned jacket, almost seemed to promise them physical safety from any serious romantic ventures by Cadets.

There was also that added degree of security of virtue thrown into the venture for the blind dates, many of whom, no doubt, were really looking to establish a relationship that might later secure them their Mrs. degrees. An added safety feature for them was that Cadets had strict limits, and it was not easy to find a protected spot that was dark while still within Cadet limits for any sharing of completely normal—but forbidden—youthful passion.

But even without girls, there was a sandy beach at Buckner, and on weekends we had access to rowboats and canoes, as well as whatever fishing gear and tackle we might want to use. There were even a few motorboats, and water-skiing was also an option, though the lines for that were so long that only a few guys ever made use of it—mostly classmates who had water-skied all their lives, of which there were some.

Just like back on the main campus of the academy, alcohol was illicit for Cadets, of course, and a major punishment awaited anyone caught with such. But Cadet rules at West Point, for some of us, were there to be broken. I remember one Saturday before supper finding my bunkmate and close friend, Buck Thompson, under the covers in his upper bunk, reading a book and giggling like a fool. Buck was a very popular and funny guy. He had been a football lineman at a midwestern college for two years, then spent two more in the army before coming to West Point, so when we arrived at Buckner he had just turned twenty-three.

He was older than most of us by at least a couple of years, and several of us were, that day, drawn like moths to the flame of his laughter. Once there, it didn't take long for us to discover that, under the covers, he had a bottle of scotch whiskey, on which he sipped while reading. And the book he read, almost unbelievably to us, was *Chaucer's Canterbury Tales*.

The Wife of Bath, no doubt, was all the more humorous when you've had a wee nip of scotch to start the story off right. We roared at his impertinence, then dragged him out of bed to get dressed for supper. He was naked, it turned out, and little short of dead drunk. As he stood, his quips from Chaucer came pouring out, and we were soon all collapsing in laughter along with Buck. Supper on Saturday night was optional, so he didn't have to be there. But we were hungry, so we left Buck to his book, his scotch, and his mirth.

Years later at graduation, we all agreed that Buck would be the first to make general in our class. Sadly, however, in November 1967, Buck would be killed in Vietnam while serving as an infantry platoon leader with the 173rd Airborne Brigade.

For our Saturday afternoon entertainment, all sorts of competitions were arranged. One I remember in particular was swimming races from one dock to another, about a hundred yards of open water. No Cadets from the swim team could compete, and I had always thought myself a very fast swimmer, easily able to beat my high school friends in the summer. In addition, I had earned a top grade in swimming when we took it as our required phys ed class during Plebe year. That was "survival swimming" more than speed, but even so, I was strong in the water.

But I was not the only cocky swimmer in the class. In fact, so many classmates had signed up so that there would be many heats of ten, and only the two fastest swimmers from each heat would move on to the finals. There, the fastest swimmers in the class would race, of whom one would emerge as class champion.

Standing at the starting line for the first heat, I felt confident that I would win, not just this first heat, but the whole competition. In fact, I thought I would be so impressive that the swim team would ask me to join them the following winter. I had foolishly bragged as much to a few classmates, so several had come to watch me.

The starting gun launched us all into the water. As I swam, I saw no one to either side and was sure I was in out in front, so I churned hard, swimming easily the fastest pace of my life. I felt good as I moved, knowing I would impress my unsuspecting classmates with my as-yet-undiscovered prowess in the water. But as I approached the finish, there was a great deal of splashing in front of me, which was confusing. Then I touched the far dock and pulled my head out of the water, not sure what was happening but suddenly realizing I hadn't won.

Not only did I not win, I got waxed. I came in dead last, and the two guys who had won the heat were already out of the water, laughing and joking with each other about who would win the finals. Given all my big talk ahead of time, I was quite embarrassed. But fortunately, my friends who had come to watch said nothing to me as they watched the next heat, so I just walked away.

Humble pie time—everybody needs some.

During the main part of the week, of course, girls on the beach and all that social stuff was frivolous, for we were really here for army training. And I must say that, although we tried to conceal our eagerness, we were all quite excited about our prospects.

By this time in our West Point careers, we were all used to getting up at dawn. That continued at Buckner, of course, and by 6:00 a.m., all five companies had formed up and started their "reveille runs." Our uniforms for this were pretty straightforward: short-sleeved white West Point T-shirt, jock strap, gray athletic shorts, cushioned socks, and combat boots. By the start of the third week, when we were in better shape, we carried our rifles when we ran.

And as we ran, we sang. There were the usual army songs—"Jody's got your girl and gone"—but we also added our own lyrics, most poking fun at the cadre or at each other. And some of the more creative lyrics were simply hilarious.

This was long before even the idea of running shoes had occurred to anyone. Once we graduated and were commissioned and assigned to a regular army unit, we knew that, like the enlisted soldiers we would lead, we would all make reveille runs wearing combat boots. So this running in boots was good preparation for our futures.

When we got back from the run, we all showered, shaved, and dressed in the olive drab fatigue uniform and the same combat boots in which we had just run. After making our beds and tidying up our personal areas for potential inspection, we went to breakfast. Then, around 8:00 a.m., formal instruction for the day began.

After graduation at the time, all Cadets had to take their commissions in one of the five so-called combat arms: infantry, armor, artillery, engineers, and signal corps. That rule has since been relaxed to allow West Pointers to take their commissions in other "support" branches, ranging from military police to chemical to aviation to transportation corps. But even being restricted as we were, we knew virtually nothing about any of the branches that would be open to us. That, however, was what we were there to learn.

Our stay at Buckner would be for nine weeks, and the first week was mostly spent marching, running, and on the rifle range, where we fired our new M-14 rifles. During Plebe year, we all had M-1 rifles that we had carried on our shoulders at parade. We could disassemble and reassemble them in the dark, and were responsible for their immaculate cleanliness: one supposed fleck of dust in barrel or breach at inspection could be the source of demerits that could easily lead to hours on the Area and consequent loss of privileges.

And just to brighten things up, we also got a heavy dose of classroom (most classes were admittedly outdoors, but still . . .) orientation in logistics support required for an army to operate. That, of course, included somewhat dry and formal blackboard exposure to maintenance of other weapons systems as well as of motor vehicles. But when the work ended, many hours of daylight remained in summertime New York state, so we flocked, almost to a man, to the beach and the boats.

10

Cold Steel

During the second week, before we really had any hands-on training, we watched two demonstrations of army units, each of which literally took our breath away.

The first was provided by a contingent from the 101st Airborne Division, which was assigned to support our class during our training at Camp Buckner. One early evening after sunset, when the horizon was darkening, our entire class was seated in bleachers on one of the firing ranges. A sergeant wearing stripes on his arms and the Screaming Eagle patch on his shoulder stood at a lectern in front of us.

"Good evening, men. I am First Sergeant James Baker. What you are about to experience should give you some idea of what it feels like to confront the full fighting power of a company of paratroopers in the assault."

He turned and gestured down range.

"About one hundred fifty meters to your front you will see a woodline. From those trees, you are about to see the one hundred sixty-eight men of A Company, Second Battalion, 502nd Infantry, of which I am the first sergeant, launch an assault coming your direction. The objective upon which they will direct their fire is the bleachers in which you are sitting. There will be no danger to you as they will only be firing blanks, and they will stop at a line some thirty meters to our front. But you should note the firepower one company can expel, and think how you might feel and what you might do if you were enemy soldiers receiving the brunt of their attack. One day, if you are very lucky, you may end up commanding such a unit, so take a good look, and drink it all in."

Then First Sergeant Baker moved to the side and a signal was passed to the men down range. Suddenly, out of the trees came a long line, left to right, of 160-odd men wearing army fatigues and helmets. Sprigs of leaves and grass sprang from their helmets and web gear as if they had grown there, and their faces were smeared with green and black camouflage stick. They all pointed their rifles and machine guns in our direction, and as they left the trees they opened fire on us and also began to roar like lions!

Jaws dropped open and, truly stunned, few of us could even move. Most of the paratroopers were firing rifles in single shots, but there were easily a dozen machine guns, maybe more, each pumping out a steady stream of fire that flashed from their muzzles. The explosive noise from their rifles and machine guns, their beast-like bellowing, and their blazing muzzle flashes were deafening, overpowering, and almost blinding, so much so that we could barely hear ourselves think. They walked toward us at a steady pace, pausing their fire while they moved only to replace spent magazines or machine gun belts, then continuing to shoot and roar. Their attack on our position was ferocious, fierce, and overwhelming.

And, to us, it was nothing short of spectacular!

Finally, they got to the marked line to our front, and the rage pouring from both their weapons and their mouths suddenly stopped. In our eyes, their green and black forms were bruised and distorted by the gray haze that had been pumped into the air from their weapons, and dead silence lasted long milliseconds as cordite nipped at our nostrils.

Man, what a rush! The emotional thrill washed over us, and without really thinking, we erupted in cheers and applause. What a fantastic show this had been!

The second demonstration would not be of brute firepower

and physical force so much as of sophisticated insertion of forces. Once again, but this time in late morning, all five Cadet companies were at the parade field and were seated in the bleachers on the side away from the lake. We had been told we were going to meet the members of a Special Forces "A" Team that had just returned from duty in South Vietnam.

There were hints of this in the *New York Times*, since President Kennedy had placed a special emphasis on the deployment of Special Forces to assist countries in the Third World that were having trouble with Communist guerrillas. But these brief stories had little detail, so we relished our first exposure to a real Special Forces "A" Team just back from engagement in such an affair.

There were perhaps forty or fifty officers already sitting at one end of the bleachers, all wearing their formal "Class A" green uniforms, and several of them had brought their well-dressed wives as well. That was unusual, but obviously the exposure to Special Forces was quite an attraction to members of the West Point staff and faculty who could make it. So obviously, with these additions to the audience, we could expect quite a show.

A small wooden lectern with a microphone had been placed in front of us, from which a captain in tiger-striped fatigues and camouflaged face and hands introduced himself to us. He told us he was the commander of an eleven-man Special Forces "A" Team that had just returned from six months' duty in South Vietnam.

While there, he told us, they had served with indigenous tribesmen called Montagnards who lived in huts built on stilts in the thickly forested mountains. This populace got everything it needed—food and water, clothing, and shelter—from within the triple-canopy jungle that was their home. And, oh, by the way, they were also fighting Communist rebels. For that, the A Team gave them military instruction as well as weapons, ammunition, radios, and medical care.

This was obviously one of the Kennedy-inspired missions, and we were readily sucked in, almost breathless as we listened.

No one asked if these tribesmen would have been fighting without American support, but at the time, such a question would not have been asked. In 1963, for all Americans, Communists were, by definition, evil, and they had to be fought whenever and wherever possible. This A Team, we learned, was just back from such an operation.

In a calm voice amplified by the microphone, the captain—an old man in his late twenties, we guessed—told us the other ten members of his A Team would arrive by different methods and assemble with him on the parade ground in front of us. He then told us to look up and we would see two of his sergeants jumping from an airplane and, just so we could see them, streaming red smoke behind them. They would be arriving by parachute demonstrating the HALO technique, which stood for "High Altitude, Low Opening."

Sure enough, we could see a tiny plane flying so high above us that we couldn't hear it. Then two dots separated from it and small red streamers grew from them. As they got lower, the streamers became red smoke that grew thicker, and as the dots grew closer, we realized they were men in free fall. Then, at what seemed like not much higher than tree-top level, both popped their parachutes and drifted down to land within twenty yards of us in the bleachers. Within seconds, each had dropped harness and lined up next to the captain.

Next, the captain said, one of the then-new Huey helicopters would arrive and hover at about thirty or forty feet above the parade ground before us and from which another of his sergeants and his only lieutenant would slide down ropes as if they were being inserted into a jungle or a city. The rest of his words were drowned out by the chopper, which arrived from above the trees to our rear and wheeled in front of us. A man was standing on the skid on either side, and as the helicopter came to a stable hover, each of them jumped up and out backward.

Each was holding on to a rope sliding through their web gear and extending from inside the open doors on each side of the helicopter. But as they fell, it quickly became apparent that something was wrong, for they had intended to slide down the rope. Instead, nothing broke their fall, and we later learned that they had somehow hooked into the wrong end of the rope.

The sergeant realized that almost right away and began pulling loops of rope out of the helicopter behind him. When he got within perhaps ten feet above the ground, the rope he was pulling suddenly grew taut and broke his fall, but he couldn't hold on to it and fell the rest of the way to the ground. He probably broke some bones, but as he lay writhing on the ground, it was clear that he was still alive.

The lieutenant, however, stayed rigid as he fell backward, bent at the waist in an L-shaped position while waiting for the rope to suddenly grow taut. It never did. He hit the parade flat on his back no more than fifty feet in front of us, and he bounced so high that, below his back, we could see a blue flash of the lake behind him. Then his legs fell flat with his torso and he didn't move again.

Two medics were standing nearby in their starched white shirts and pants, apparently just for show. But they scrambled onto the field to tend the two men, as did a major who, it turned out, was a doctor watching from the stands with his wife, but ran onto the field in his dress green uniform. As they tended to the men, the helicopter disappeared, and soon an ambulance that had been parked nearby was there. Once the two men, the two medics, and the doctor were aboard, the lights and siren came on and it sped away.

Our Yearling class was still standing in open-mouthed shock. This was no elaborate trick, we all knew that. But what had just happened? Had we really just watched a man jump to his death, obviously not meaning to do so, from a helicopter hovering fifty feet above us? We were still rattled when the captain's calm voice startled us all.

"If you will direct your attention to the far side of the lake, you will see what looks like a dead tree trunk floating this way. It is actually a camouflaged boat being pushed through the water by two more of my sergeants who are . . ."

What? The second-in-command of this A Team, the lieutenant with whom you had recently completed six months of combat service in Vietnam, just fell from a helicopter in a tragic accident and may well be dead. But you are so calm, cool, and collected that you instantly realized your men are in an ambulance under the care of a doctor and two medics while speeding to a hospital, that you can do nothing more for them, and that the mission must be performed! And you are able to just continue the lesson plan with no interruption? Wow! What a man! That was just the sort of calm professionalism in a crisis to which we all aspired.

A few minutes later, a staff car arrived and whisked the captain away, obviously to see about his men. The rest of the Special Forces presentation was canceled, and we were all released and ended up spending the rest of the afternoon back in the barracks or, for those who had the stomach, on the beach.

We later asked officers about the medical situation of the two men who had fallen from the Huey, and although it seemed to us that the lieutenant who had bounced so high right in front of us was almost certainly dead, we never got a straight answer. But lying on our cots or on the sand, we brand-new Yearlings talked together in hushed tones and truly marveled at the captain. What a man! Dared we even aspire to one day have that professional presence, that sangfroid in the face of professional and personal tragedy? We couldn't answer that, of course, but it was a magnificent display of professionalism under pressure, and a goal to which we all, to a greater or lesser extent, aspired.

11

Army Field Training

After those two demonstrations and others less stunning, each of the five companies began to rotate through specific training with each of the five branches. And the last week, the capstone of our Camp Buckner training, would be what was known as "Recondo Week."

We would be supported throughout our stay by a large contingent of the 101st Airborne Division from Fort Campbell, Kentucky, and they clearly included the fierce men of A Company, Second of the 502nd, who had just riddled us with imaginary bullets while we sat rooted to our seats in the stands. These "Screaming Eagle" soldiers would act both as instructors during branch orientation and training, and then later as our "Aggressors," the men who would fill the role of our adversaries and against whom we would operate during Recondo Week.

For all branches, training started with dry lectures on how that branch was ideally used in wartime. When the infantry course started, for instance, we first learned its theoretical operations in conjunction with armor and artillery. But on the second day we got down and dirty, first with hand-to-hand combat in a sawdust pit, later fighting each other with pugil sticks while wearing helmets and padded gloves. Then we crawled under strung barbed wire or over rolls of concertina wire, navigated through thickly wooded hilly terrain with just a map and a compass, dug foxholes, trenches, and latrines, and learned various routines and traditions that would allow us to flourish with infantry, the "Queen of Battle." That training was sometimes exhilarating fun, but it was also quite exhausting work.

Armor training took place in an open plain on the west side of the reservation, and after a certain amount of lecture and dry-run rehearsal, we were allowed to climb on board M-48 tanks and operate them, down to filling the roles of each of the four crew members (driver, gunner, loader, tank commander). There was always one active-duty sergeant or officer on board each tank just as a safety measure, and not only did we drive them cross-country, we also took them to a range, where we got to fire their two machine guns and even the long tube that came out of the turret, their 90 mm main gun. To us as future officers, neophytes all, just climbing aboard such a steel monster and then taking our places as crew members and operating it in open country was nothing short of thrilling.

Artillery training occurred in another open area near the tank training ground, and both the tank main guns and artillery pieces were fired at the same targets on a safe range. Again, there was a certain amount of tedium that was required for us to learn how to load powder charges inside artillery canisters, how to adjust fire, and other technical details that ate up time we wanted to spend firing on the range. But soon enough we were able to do just that, and we served as gun crew members, then as forward observers, and finally in the Fire Direction Center, where we determined charges, ranges, directions, and other details required before firing the guns. We burned a lot of powder and blew up a lot of truck hulks that had been placed down range for that purpose. Firing the guns was fun, but it was also deafening.

Although it was included as a "combat arm," Signal Corps training was not a branch that "put metal down range," so to speak, and it was normally considered to be less dangerous to its soldiers than infantry, armor, or artillery—unless, of course, you were doing something particularly hazardous like laying commo wire on a battlefield. But during our training with Signal, we first learned how to tune and calibrate PRC-10 radios, thirty-pound monsters that designated enlisted men carried on their backs in combat while staying close to the man who would use them, their squad/platoon leader or company commander. We also learned how to lay communication wire and how to use electrical or pedal-powered generators to produce enough juice for us to communicate. This was a branch that, should we choose it after graduation, would require considerable technical training. Even so, we learned a lot about communication we had never even suspected, and that might well be of use to us in combat, should that ever occur.

And finally we were trained in the operations of the Corps of Engineers. Like the Signal Corps, the Engineers were considered a combat branch, but in the peacetime army we expected to enter, that would involve little personal danger. Oh, sure, putting a bridge across a river in combat could be very hazardous indeed. During peace time, however, the Corps of Engineers was focused on domestic projects like flood control and building and maintaining dams and bridges, particularly within the Mississippi Valley. But based on its history, the Corps of Engineers had a certain cachet that the other branches lacked.

Because the U.S. Military Academy had started as a school of engineering, the Corps of Engineers had retained much of its sway at West Point, particularly in the academic curriculum: no matter which branch of service a Cadet might choose, every graduate was a trained engineer. And it was very demanding technically, even more so than the Signal Corps.

Probably because of that, after graduation the Corps of Engineers was usually chosen by what was considered academically to be the cream of West Point's annual crop. For us at Buckner, training by the Corps of Engineers dealt with what you would need to build or to blow up a bridge, a wall, a berm, a canal, and so on. This was intellectually stimulating work that appealed more to some—the smartest guys in math and engineering—than to others.

When branches were chosen at graduation in those days, it was done by class rank. Each branch had to accept a minimum number and could not exceed a maximum number, both specified ahead of time. Traditionally, men near the top of each class academically would choose the Corps of Engineers, and its quota was usually filled before the first 20 percent had made their choices. Other than that, the choice of branch came down to what attracted each Cadet. And those choices were often formed while new Yearlings were first being exposed to them there at Camp Buckner.

Camp Buckner's training ended with Recondo Week, during which each platoon of twenty Yearlings would operate independently somewhere on the vast reservation of wooded hills that surrounded us. We wore steel helmets and carried backpacks in which were one waterproof poncho, one woolen blanket, one shelter-half tarp, and one C-ration meal in a small cardboard box, as well as dry socks and underwear. Hanging from our web gear we carried canteens, smoke grenades, and ammunition pouches.

Referred to by upperclassmen as "Mini-Ranger School," Recondo would consist of one week of constant movement on supposed "missions" with very few hours of sleep allowed each night and very little food. It was a genuine trial. Each Cadet would rotate through the position of patrol leader, and as such he would be required to follow a specified azimuth through the woods for a number of kilometers.

Azimuth was followed with a compass, and distance would be measured by counting paces. When he arrived at his objective, the patrol leader *du jour* was supposed to find an ammunition box painted orange and nailed to a tree at shoulder level. Inside that box (twelve inches long, six inches high, four inches wide) he would find further directions: another azimuth and another distance. Patrol leadership would then rotate to another Cadet.

Each patrol was accompanied by a lieutenant or a sergeant from the 101st, and these men would grade the patrol leader on his movements. Needless to say, since we were brand new at this game, a lot of those ammo boxes took a long time to find. These patrols lasted for most of the day and night, with Cadets almost constantly moving. We would each be issued one more C-ration meal around midday. We could eat it whenever we chose, but we only got one meal each day. In addition, the Cadets on patrol were only allowed to sleep between two and three hours each night.

And every third or fourth "mission," we would be ambushed by "aggressors" from the 101st, all firing blanks. We returned fire with blanks, but then scattered to reassemble at a "rally point" near the last mission target. If we were captured by the aggressors, we would miss getting our C-ration meal for that day and would also not be allowed to sleep. In addition, being captured was considered very bad form. So when ambushed, we fired a few blank rounds, and unless called forward by the patrol leader, we all ran like hell back the way we had come.

As the days passed, the result was an ever-increasing number of very tired and very hungry Cadets. It never got as bad as Beast, though we were seriously hungry. But, we later realized, it was only through such stress that each of us began to learn how much we could actually do under pressure. And we also began to understand our own limits as well, to know and anticipate what we could *not* physically do, which was perhaps just as important if not more so.

Then, before we knew it, Recondo was over. The next day, we packed our gear, said a fond adieu to the lake and its beach, and got on the bus back to the main academy grounds. And within a few days, as we drew our books and our class schedule, that bubble of delusion, after the end of Plebe year the previous June, that it was "all over," was quickly popped. Not only was it not "all over," but we also realized that we still had three more years before it would truly be all over—at least as far as the baggage of constant strain carried every day by every West Point Cadet was concerned.

12

Yearlings

The weather at West Point in the fall is gorgeous. By mid-October, the trees that carpet both banks of the upper Hudson Valley had burst into scarlet and pumpkin flame. Rays of soft sunlight warmed our shoulders as we paraded, while even the lightest of breezes flashed tongues of fire through the trees ringing the Plain. If you could pay any attention to it, the physical environment at West Point was splendid. But that was a very big "if" that eluded all Cadets of all classes nearly all the time.

That fall, the ranks of the staff and faculty at West Point were stiffened by men returning from Vietnam. There they had been "Advisors" to the South Vietnamese Army. At the time, that was the only "war" in which the U.S. Army was engaged, even though American soldiers were not actively engaged in combat. Still, they were close enough to hear gunfire, and to train/advise South Vietnamese forces that were doing the actual fighting. To us, back in well-protected somewhat-upper New York State while training to become officers ourselves, that was very heady stuff indeed.

And uncomfortable news from Vietnam kept appearing in the *New York Times*. President Diem was unmarried and so the de facto First Lady of the Republic of Vietnam was Madame Nhu, the wife of his younger brother, Ngo Diem Nhu. After the first monk had set himself afire, that august lady said that if there were to be more Buddhist barbecues, she would happily supply the matches. That struck us as a rather odd comment, to say the least, and Madame Nhu was soon known in the American press as the Dragon Lady.

Over the next few months, Diem's brother Nhu conducted raids on pagodas in which hundreds of Buddhists died. This resulted in five more Buddhist monks consecutively dying self-immolated fiery deaths while Kennedy pressed Diem for change. Diem mouthed the right words but once again did nothing, claiming Communist infiltration into Buddhist monk affairs. Then on November 2, 1963, in the middle of a political coup, Diem and his younger brother Nhu, Madame Nhu's husband, were shot dead inside an armored personnel carrier on a street in Saigon.

This was terribly confusing to us, and we tended to just dismiss all such news as internal politics we would never understand in a strange foreign land. And anyway, it was an unwanted interference with our norms, for autumn at West Point meant one social focus more important than any other: football. The Army coach in his second year was Paul Dietzel, who had won a national championship at Louisiana State University, and the Army team in those pre-NFL-Big-Bucks days was routinely a top-ten team in the nation. But of all the games we played, no Cadet passion, no naked emotion even approached that felt and openly shown when we played Navy.

That's not at all unusual, for both schools attracted the same candidates for training and introduction into hoped-for military careers. Admission offices at both academies sought young men with excellent grades in high school, top scores in aptitude tests, marked success in athletics, and virtually unblemished physical health. The result was that Cadets and midshipmen were peas out of the same pod. And as the only colleges whose students were necessarily well-rounded leaders-in-training, athletic competition between the two of us was ferocious.

But on Friday, November 22, 1963, as pressure and emotion built before that fall's Army-Navy game, our nation was stabbed in the heart when President John F. Kennedy was assassinated.

Although he had served in the navy rather than the army during World War II, he was an undeniable war hero, and whatever the color of his uniform, to us Cadets he was a demi-god. No, to most of us, he was a true god. So how could this be? Almost to a man, except perhaps for a few of his fervent political enemies from the Deep South, we were crushed.

The Army-Navy football game had been scheduled to be played the following Saturday, November 30, but this national shock changed everything. Given the death of the president, the military services all observed the national thirty-day period of mourning. Because it was clear right away that there would be no official celebrations of any sort during this period, we expected that the Navy game would be canceled. And while no formal statements about this were made for several days, the one game that enlivened us more than any other was almost forgotten.

On Monday, we went to class and both Cadets and faculty were in a deep funk. It was not encouraging that the quarterback for the Navy team, Roger Staubach, had become a national sports hero, and on the next day, Tuesday, November 26, he was awarded the Heisman Trophy. But that same day, we learned Jackie Kennedy had announced that her late husband had been such a great fan of the Army-Navy football game that she asked that it be played in his honor. That was all it took, and so the Army-Navy game was rescheduled for Saturday, December 7.

That news lifted the pall over the academy somewhat, but even so, we remained depressed and sort of drifted through our classes. And there were no bonfires, no pep rallies, none of the usual spirit-building pre–Navy game festivities. Navy was than undefeated and ranked No. 2 nationally, behind only No. 1 Texas. Army had lost two games early in the season, but was still ranked No. 6 in the country. The teams of the two academies were so evenly matched, then, that it was decided that whichever team won in Philadelphia would play Texas in the Cotton Bowl on January 1, 1964.

And we fully expected to beat Navy. Our confidence was so

high, in fact, that we began writing to families (pay phones were painfully expensive and little used except for girlfriends) about the upcoming trip to Dallas. This awareness that we might go to a Bowl game lifted our spirits somewhat, and soon enough it was time for us to get up extra-early, march down to the train station by the river, and climb onto the train to Philly.

On the ride down, our excitement grew. Yeah, they had Staubach, but we had a pretty great quarterback too, Rollie Stichweh, and we thought he could win the day for us. This time, after having lost for four consecutive years, we knew we had the team that could win.

After we detrained in the rail yards near the stadium, we Black Knights of the Hudson formed up by companies, then marched toward the stadium. A cold wind swept us along, but we ignored it, singing army fight songs and building our confidence with every step. Then we stopped in the shadows outside the stadium, and the army band moved to our front.

There was a pause for a few minutes and we took that time to close and dress our ranks. We were in a tight gray formation, brass buttons shining down the front of our long overcoats, capes thrown jauntily back over our shoulders, brims of our caps pulled down so they almost touched our noses. We were America's Spartan warriors, come to do battle with her Athenian sailors: may the best men win.

Then the order came to march. Ahead, there were somewhat muffled cheers from the 100,000 fans awaiting us inside the amphitheater, but the only noise we heard as we moved was from the brass and drums, their heavy beat keeping us all uniformly in step. Then we turned a corner, still tightly packed together, and our first ranks stopped just out of view of the crowd. After a pause, the band struck up "On Brave Old Army Team," and we stepped out suddenly, seen from the stands as a wild gray river disgorging relentlessly onto the sun-soaked green tapestry. The crowd erupted in a wall of noise that washed over our suddenly sun-splashed faces.

We marched boldly onto the blazing emerald lists, and when we halted, our formation covered most of the field. The Middies were already in the stands, and after a loud "Beat Navy!" from us, we flooded up into our side. Then we turned to face them and we became two enormous bands of barbarian berserkers howling defiance amid mass cheers at each other, with the clearly thrilled and raucous civilian fans shouting hosannas for both teams.

Then the players came out onto the battlefield, and the Navy team had "Drive for Five" emblazoned on the backs of their jerseys, this referring to the possibility of five consecutive wins over Army that lay before them that day. To the Army team, that was a mocking insult, and they were personally enraged. Both coaches reminded their teams they were playing to honor a slain president, and that they should play a game worthy of him. But for Army, this latest insult had moved things beyond the normal rivalry, and they wanted to smear the turf with Navy blood.

The game started well enough for us, with Army jumping to a 7–0 lead. But the battle on the field was fierce, and that surprised even knowledgeable people. University of Texas coach Darrell Royal was in the press box to scout both teams, as one of them would be his Cotton Bowl opponent, and his comment was "They're trying to maim each other!" Army stopped Navy with a goal-line stand. But Staubach was as good as advertised, and Navy came back with three touchdowns. They led 21–7 with ten minutes left in the fourth quarter.

Then Rollie Stichweh took over. First he led Army in a long drive and they scored a touchdown, then went for two and made it. With the score 21–15, Army made an onside kick, and it was Rollie Stichweh who recovered the ball. Again, he led Army down the field, and with 2 minutes and 43 seconds left, Army had a first and 10 on the Navy 8-yard line. Three more runs got to the 1-yard line, but the noise from the crowd was so loud that neither Stichweh nor his teammates could hear anything.

In those days, Army had no silent snap signal or anything

like it, and the team depended on hearing the count from their quarterback. They had never experienced anything like this deafening noise. It was fourth down with a yard to go for a winning touchdown, and Stichweh looked at the referees, pleading with them to stop the clock so his team could hear. But Navy partisans kept up the roar, and then, suddenly, time had expired and the game was over: referees blew their whistles and waved their arms, and a Navy player grabbed the ball and ran off with it.

The Army team stood there, shocked and blinking in disbelief. The Corps of Cadets in the stands really couldn't believe what had just happened. We all felt cheated out of a chance for one more play that, we knew, would have scored a touchdown and so won the game for us, 22–21. But instead, the finger of fate had touched the Army team, and Navy really had won, 21–15.

Drive for Five, indeed.

The blow endured after we got back to our Rockbound Highland Home, as West Point has long been remembered by her graduated sons, but we struggled and overcame it. Our Navy-hating emotions dissipated as sport took center stage, and intramurals covered a wide array of choices: Bob Lowry and Mike Brennan played basketball, Mike Mewhinney wrestled, Deme Clainos boxed, Art Mosley played squash, and I skied—or rather, I learned how to ski. But most other Cadets were in the same boat, so ski races were for the most part between utter tyros.

Christmas leave came and passed, and then we were all back. There were several feet of snow covering the Plain by January, though we still had our several-times-weekly parades. But in winter, we marched inside Central Area in what were called "band box parades."

On January 30, 1964, we read of a bloodless coup that had taken place in Vietnam, after which the government was run by a General Khanh, whoever he was. The number of U.S. Army "advisors" serving with South Vietnamese troops was steadily increasing, though American casualties were reported as "light." Still, any casualties at all were a cause for concern.

13

Goethe

That spring, Deme told me and Art Mosley that he could get us on a weekend trip to New York City, free hotel, free dinner Saturday and Sunday at the hotel, and free theater tickets if we were interested. And of course we were! What did we have to do?

It was pretty simple, actually. His friend Clair Thurston, whom he had met in the Math Forum during Plebe year, was a big shot in the German Club, and they had scheduled a trip to New York City to watch a performance of Goethe's *Faust*. And while it was an important piece of German culture, it ran for nearly four hours.

It seems that a lieutenant colonel instructor in the German department at West Point had been a guest at a recent cocktail party at the German embassy in Washington DC. After a few drinks, he told the German ambassador how popular German culture was among Cadets. He may even have exaggerated a bit, but he thought this just a polite compliment to his host. To his great surprise, however, the German ambassador had sent him thirty-six tickets to *Faust*, which would be staged in German in New York City. A bit nonplussed, he kept six tickets for himself, two other professors, and their wives, then gave the rest of the tickets to the German Club, with instructions that they were all to be used. But other than Clair Thurston, there were only about a dozen Cadets who were both club members and wanted to see the play.

So the German Club was caught a bit flat-footed. The colonel couldn't just give the tickets back to the ambassador, as not using them might be seen as some sort of diplomatic insult, which West Point would simply not do. So they were looking for Cadets to use them, and if we wanted to spend a Saturday night in New York City, the German Embassy would foot the bill for everything: free tickets, free hotel, free food; all we had to do was join the German Club. And for this embarrassment-saving trip, joining the German Club didn't even mean we had to speak German—all we had to do was to go through the motions and sign up for the trip.

Mose and I did so, and pretty quickly, other Cadets heard about it and all the tickets were gone. Having been released from the mandatory Saturday parade because of the trip—yet another goody for a Cadet—we left on a bus early Saturday morning wearing our readily identifiable Dress Gray Cadet uniforms. There were also three officers on the trip, all instructors of German, and they had brought their wives with them. One of them, a lieutenant colonel, was the officer in charge (OIC) of this trip, and whatever else we did, we had to avoid being singled out by him. We felt pretty safe, however, because we didn't take German, so he had no idea who we were. But mostly, we were grateful to Deme's buddy, Clair Thurston, who had given us this splendid opportunity for a free night in New York City.

When we got off the bus around noon, we were greeted by some guy in a dark suit and tie who spoke to us in German. The Cadets who did speak German laughed and we just followed their lead, smiling and nodding our heads as appropriate. He led us into a big hotel where we were given keys and took our small overnight bags up to our rooms. Then we met downstairs and were ushered into a dining room, where we had a heavy German meal.

Soon enough, we got back on the bus and drove into the theater district for the two o'clock show, which, with two intermissions, would last until almost 6:00 p.m. After that, we would be released on the town, where we were expected to buy supper on our own and then do whatever we wanted for the rest of the night. But Deme and Art and I had no interest at all in watching a play in German, and we had already agreed on the bus that, once the play started, we would make our ways to the back of the theater, find an exit, and then split. Hell, rather than spending four hours in a dark theater listening to a play in a language we didn't even understand, we could be doing something productive, like drinking beer and trying to pick up girls!

When we found our seats in the theater, they were all in one block of three rows on the left side of the theater. The three officers and their wives were sitting in the front row of the three while Deme and Art and I, to our great good fortune, were two rows behind them. Then the lights went down, the curtain came up, and we found ourselves in an aristocratic salon in eighteenth-century Germany. Heavy drapes, thick rugs, ornate furniture, candelabra, the whole Goethe thing. The characters, both men and women, were wearing the clothing of nobles, including white period wigs. And when they began to speak to each other in German, to us it might as well have been in Greek.

Deme was sitting on my right, and Art was beyond him at the end of the row. After about ten minutes, Deme nudged my arm and I looked his way. In the dim light, I could see Art lean forward, then motion with his head toward the rear. I nodded, and the three of us stood up and quietly walked into the aisle, then turned and walked toward the back of the theater. I was last in line, and suddenly, we stopped.

I could see Art speaking in hushed tones with an usher, who blocked our way. Then he turned and joined Deme and me, speaking in a whisper.

"He says we can't go out through the lobby for some reason I didn't understand. But there's an exit sign over there, on the side, so let's go there."

Art simply turned right and walked behind the rear-most row of seats toward a red EXIT sign on the wall with an arrow pointing down what looked like a dark corridor. Once there, we turned right and started going back down the carpeted slope of the floor toward the front of the theater. But a wall separated us from the rest of the audience and we were then no longer in their sight, so we pressed on in the dark.

A hundred feet ahead on our left another EXIT sign glowed dully above a set of double doors. As we approached it, however, we suddenly realized that we had walked beyond the end of the wall separating us from the theater seats, and the entire audience could have seen us had they looked. But they were all caught up in the play and we were just shadows moving in the dark.

Art was in front, and the double doors had a waist-level bar across each of them on which you pushed to open it. An extra-wide double door, we assumed, probably for stage props and so on. But beyond it, we were sure, was another dark corridor that would lead us back to the lobby and then out to the hot city! So Art leaned on the bar of the nearest door and pushed it open.

The door screeched like a vampire as it swung back, turning every head in the theater our way as it simultaneously seemed like a thousand suns lit us up. Unhappily, the door led directly out onto the street, where cars rushed by as sunlight poured into the formerly dark theater along with the sounds and smells of downtown New York City.

We froze for a second, not sure what to do, and it seemed like the entire world came to a stop. Then the three of us bolted through the door as best we could, our uniforms leaving no doubt for the audience that we were West Point Cadets, and we ran like hell. We were trying to smother our laughter when we got around the first corner, and if the OIC decided to find out who we were, we could be in big trouble. So we kept running until we got to a subway stop, paid our ten-cent fare, and rode into Greenwich Village, where we had a very hot time that afternoon, evening, and night.

As it turned out, the West Point officers at the German play had just ignored our early departure, and we never heard any official word about it. Before we got on the bus to return to West Point on Sunday, however, Deme apologized to Clair Thurston. But Clair said that when the door had opened, the light and traffic noise were such a shock to everyone that they thought it was some kind of stage malfunction or something to do with the theater. He said he never saw Cadets going through the open door, so we should forget about it. We did.

14

SPNSS, 0030 Hours, 21 November 1965

Behind us the Marine guards were talking to someone new, then laughing together. After that, a uniformed Marine—we assumed the new one we had just heard talking—walked past us on the sidewalk on his way into the Security Station. If he had looked to his right as he went by, he would have seen the five of us sprawled on our faces, for we had nowhere to hide in the bright glare of the floodlight that shone on us from somewhere above the guard post. But instead, he kept turning his head to the left and looking back at the pretty girls still talking to the Marines.

It seemed to take forever for this new Marine to get out of sight, and we dared not look, but we could hear the girls laughing openly with the two guards. Then Deme and Mike were back on their feet and cautiously approached Billy XIV, his great rack of horns still shaking ominously. But when they first touched him, he stayed immobile. Obviously, he thought they were just more of the regular guys who visited him to feed him and groom him, and he never moved as Deme got his loop over the great horns and around his neck.

Then it was Mike's turn, and things went well as he got the rope loop over the long left horn. But as he tried to stretch it around and over the right horn, the goat suddenly stepped his right foot through the loop. Mike tried to stay calm as he reached down and pulled on his leg, but then sudden bright light washed over us, and we were all back on the ground.

15

Cow Year

During the following summer, we went to Germany for thirty days, where we served as junior lieutenants in U.S. Army units assigned there, as part of the Army Orientation Training program. Then we all took two weeks' leave and traveled through Europe on our own, each of us in the company of a handful of classmates.

But even in Europe, news of the war in Vietnam was heating up and making us ever more aware. On August 2 and 4, 1964, two American destroyers, the *Maddox* and the *Turner Joy*, were reportedly attacked by North Vietnamese torpedo boats in the Tonkin Gulf. Within hours after the supposed second attack (which Americans would learn decades later never took place), President Johnson launched retaliatory air attacks on North Vietnamese naval facilities. And a few days later, he got Congress to pass the Tonkin Gulf Resolution.

That congressional measure authorized the president's use of "all necessary measures" to repel any armed attacks against U.S. forces and to prevent further aggression. It also said maintenance of peace and security in Southeast Asia was vital to American interests and to world peace.

To us, this was so much legal gobbledygook, but clearly it freed the president's hand. Even so, combat on the ground in South Vietnam did not yet involve American fighting forces. But within less than a year, that was to change.

After our European duty followed by vacation, we found ourselves back at West Point in the fall for another semester of soul-draining academics. West Point had just been scheduled by Congress to expand from 2,500 men to 4,400 over the next few years in order to match the Naval Academy's enrollment. To accommodate this, a structural change was made so that our two regiments were expanded to four and the company designations were changed to accommodate this: G-1 became A-3, B-2 became H-4, and so on. But since our class size would not change, this was only a paper game that made absolutely no difference to us, and we just chalked it up to another instance of form over substance

The weather was gorgeous as usual, and on Saturday and Sunday afternoons, bands of pretty girls seemed to just float around the Plain, many of them undoubtedly hoping to somehow meet a Cadet. But by then, most of us had steady girlfriends, many of whom came up for the weekend, so the attraction of meeting some babe who was a complete stranger had lessened dramatically. And within our closed society, which we could not leave either after class or after supper, that meant we focused our energies on the success of the football team. And as usual, one game mattered more to us than any other.

Leading up to The Game, Navy's Roger Staubach and Army's Rollie Stichweh were both seniors. In games with other teams throughout the season, they each performed deeds of derring-do that were splashed across the country's sports pages. Then in late November, we went down to Philadelphia once again for our annual duel. But this time, the fates finally turned our way, and we won! The score was an unusual 11–8, but in the aftermath, *Sports Illustrated* said, "Stichweh outplayed Staubach as no player has before." And that, finally, was enough for us.

Then true "Gloom Period" set in with a vengeance: gray buildings, gray skies, gray uniforms, gray lives. We were required to be in our rooms, whether cramming from books or trying to solve problems with slide rules, every night but Saturday without fail. The weather was unusually cold and the snow drifts on the Plain grew ever deeper. The wind coming down the Hudson seemed to slash through our heavy woolen overcoats and kept us indoors as much as possible. But our options there were generally limited to being in our rooms studying, in class learning, in the gym playing sports, or occasionally on weekends, and all too rarely, in an illicitly parked car with a girlfriend trying to score.

Through the fall and winter, the war in Southeast Asia had just kept on simmering. On December 20, we read in the *Times*, there had been another coup in Vietnam. This time, a new group of generals took over, led by the young and dashing-looking Air Marshal Ky. He named himself premier, which really meant nothing to us. In any case, he was a new face, and at first, Americans were drawn by his good looks alone. But the government of South Vietnam seemed all the more to us at West Point like that of some banana republic, with rotating gangs of generals funded by Uncle Sam to stave off Communism, whatever that meant.

After we got back from Christmas vacation in early January 1965, we read in the *New York Times* an official Department of Defense year-end summary informing us that, of the 23,000 U.S. troops in Vietnam during 1964, 140 had been killed and 1,138 wounded. There were not yet any American combat units in Vietnam, and the dead and wounded had all been "advisors," which, we thought, meant little more than observers from a distance.

But those casualty figures quickly disabused us of such folly. We were to graduate a year and a half later, and it looked increasingly like we might all find ourselves over there in positions of personal danger. And that meant *real* danger, as in alive as a survivor or dead by gunfire.

That spring President Johnson moved with frightening alacrity. After a request from the commanding general of U.S. forces in Vietnam, he sent 3,500 Marines to protect the American air base in Danang, the first deployment of American fighting troops to Vietnam. And that commanding general was none other than William C. Westmoreland, who had been our superintendent at West Point during Plebe year and Mike Brennan's gracious host for Christmas dinner. The Marines arrived on March 8, 1965, with an initial mission of defending an American installation from attack by Communist forces, and nothing more. But that mission was to expand significantly in a very short time.

Meanwhile, trouble was brewing in the Caribbean. On April 24, 1965, a military coup in the Dominican Republic attempted to overthrow the ruling civilian government in favor of a deposed former president. But not all of the military supported this, and within days a full-fledged civil war was being fought there. On April 28 the U.S. ambassador asked for Marines to protect the embassy and help evacuate innocent bystanders. Four hundred Marines were dispatched for that purpose. Then on April 30 elements of the Eighty-Second Airborne Division began to arrive.

By May 1 the extreme left had begun taking over leadership of the rebel force, including avowed Communists trained in Cuba and other Communist countries. There was a period of intense fighting, and the Eighty-Second waded into it, establishing a neutral corridor some sixteen miles long between the rebels and government forces. In addition to defending themselves against snipers and assisting in evacuation, these soldiers also began to distribute food and medical supplies to innocent victims in the capital city of Santo Domingo.

On May 10, Second Lt. Charles Hutchison, who had graduated from West Point in 1964, was leading his platoon of the Eighty-Second in Santo Domingo. Their company had been harassed that day by a rebel 50-caliber machine gun firing on them from a cupola atop a two-story building. Hutch, as he was known at West Point, led his platoon in an attempt to quiet the gun. Darting from doorway to doorway as the machine gun kept firing at them, they grew ever closer to their target. Then one of his men was hit and fell into the street, screaming and clutching at his wounds. Without thinking, Hutch ran to rescue his fallen soldier. But before he got there, he took a bullet in the side of his head and died instantly.

Cow Year

The fighting in the Dominican Republic was largely over by the end of the summer of 1965. During those few months of combat, 24 American soldiers were killed and another 156 were wounded. To us Cadets back at West Point, this was grave news. Hutch had been a rather tall but quiet Cadet, and he had invested himself entirely in the basketball team. We all knew him from his play on the courts, where he had been somewhat of a star. He was buried in Riverview cemetery in Apollo, Pennsylvania, so there was no formal ceremony at the academy. Still, his was the first combat death of anyone who had been a Cadet with us, and it was sobering, to say the least.

While that local affair was distracting the American public, our nation's participation in a war on the other side of the world was slowly building. Less than two months after the Marines arrived in Vietnam on March 8, a U.S. Army fighting force would arrive in Vietnam in the form of the 173rd Airborne Brigade, also some 3,500 strong. And over that summer, many more Marines and soldiers would arrive in Vietnam.

That war was suddenly brought more to our personal attention on July 8, 1965, when the next man who had worn Cadet gray with us died in combat. On that night, Lt. Jack Eitel, who graduated from West Point in 1963 and had taken his commission in the Marine Corps, was serving with G Company, Second Battalion, Fourth Marines. As best we could learn, Eitel was setting up a night ambush with his platoon when a massive failure of communication occurred. In full dark, for whatever reasons, Lieutenant Eitel and a private first class with him were moving when they were mistaken for enemy soldiers and shot dead by their own men.

Jack had been a Firsty when we were Plebes, and that first year he and Mosley had been in the Dialectic Society together. But none of the rest of us had played sports or engaged in other extracurricular activities with him, nor had we been in his Cadet company, so none of the six of us really knew him personally. Still, it was a heavy blow that hit home hard.

First Hutch, then Jack. Who would be next? For all we knew, even though graduation was still a year away, we saw the reality before us that any of us might, all too soon, find ourselves hurled from that same train. Suddenly, as the cold realities of our own potential deaths in combat began to sink in, the fantasies about becoming soldiers at war were no longer quite as attractive or romantic as they had been. No, in time of war, the army was a grim business.

16

Firsty Year

In mid-September 1965, our senior year at West Point, I spent a week in the hospital with a bad case of the flu. And in the bed next to me, also with the flu, was—surprise!—Deme Clainos. We were both a bit on the wild side, and now that we were Firsties ourselves, we wanted to do something adventurous and exciting, something that would make the rest of the Corps sit up and take notice.

At first, we had no idea what that could be. But after talking about possibilities for a while, it turned out that, before even coming to West Point, we had both heard about the theft of the Navy goat by West Point Cadets in 1955. And that was it!

Traditionally, neither Army nor Navy plays a football game on the weekend before their annual face-off, and in the first half of the twentieth century, that was a major, much-watched-on-television contest. Indeed, during the twenty years between 1944 and 1964, two Navy players and three from Army had won Heisman trophies, marking them as the best football players in the land.

By the late sixties, however, the Vietnam War and its direct threat of personal death or serious injury had deterred many young men from attending the academies. And even after that war ended, the suddenly booming popularity of the NFL promised enormous paychecks for recently graduated college football stars. While they were still in high school, therefore, any lad who thought he could win a football scholarship to college usually also had a dream of big bucks and social glory in the NFL.

Consequently, these young men seldom even looked at the academies, which required their graduates to serve four years in uniform, an added burden that effectively put the NFL out of the picture for them. In addition, graduates of the Air Force Academy or the Naval Academy faced challenging futures, but as young officers, few of them would hear gunfire exchanged in anger. For those who graduated from the Military Academy at West Point, on the other hand, personal combat was often one of the rites of passage. That helps explain how and why, since the early 1970s, Army football team records have fallen from levels of national prominence and championship seasons to middle-of-the-pack mediocrity. Or worse.

But to West Point Cadets in 1965, that evolution was still in the as-yet-unseen and undreamed-of future. The 1955 theft of the Navy goat, ten years earlier, Deme and I had both read, had occurred on the Saturday night before the Army-Navy football game. But the Cadets who pulled it off had stolen it from the unguarded pen in which it was kept on the wide-open-to-the-public campus of the Naval Academy in Annapolis.

Since then, for the two weeks before the Army-Navy football game, the goat was routinely transferred to the nearby Severna Park Naval Security Station (SPNSS), the highest security installation of the U.S. Navy. The goat was kept there in a pen attached to the rear of the main guard post manned 24/7 by Marines who, we were told, had orders to shoot trespassers on sight, and shoot to kill.

But we didn't really believe that and were not deterred at all. Deme and I decided we could steal the goat ourselves, Marine guards be damned! So once out of the hospital, we began to recruit other close-friend classmates.

We were very careful to try to recruit only guys we thought had the spine to attempt what would clearly be a high-risk effort. And indeed, from inside West Point, such a feat did look like some sort of "Mission Impossible." If we tried and were caught, we knew there would be very hell to pay. But if we were able to succeed and bring the Navy goat back with us to West Point, then to other Cadets, to our rival midshipmen at Annapolis, and even to the outside world, that feat would be seen as a West Point triumph close to very heaven!

At the time, as a condition of graduation, many civilian colleges required their seniors, in concert with a faculty adviser, to write some sort of thesis about something they had there learned. Because West Point was then exclusively a school of engineering, no such thesis requirement existed. But if we could find a way to break into the Severna Park Naval Security Station, distract the Marine guards so as to be able to abduct the Navy goat, then bring him back to West Point, why, what better demonstration could there be of our military prowess than carrying off a raid into the enemy's most inner sanctum and making off with their most treasured symbol?

In our efforts to recruit classmates, we found that most of the men we approached simply dismissed the idea out of hand, most of them ridiculing the possibility that we might even try. But by late October, we had assembled a team of eight. One of these was Adam Acton, whose father was an accountant in Ponderosa, Maryland, only about ten miles from the SPNSS. We decided to use their home as our forward operating base, and Adam's father agreed to it.

Then, through Adam, we asked his father to take his two younger sisters to try to see the Navy goat on the afternoon of Sunday, November 14, the very day that the Naval Academy ·moved him there for added security over the following two weeks. We were worried about that security, and we wanted Mr. Acton to make a preliminary reconnaissance run for us, just to see what we would face. But before they did so, unwelcome news from Vietnam stopped us.

On November 8, 1965, two more members of the class of 1964 were killed in Vietnam, and at the time of their deaths, both had been platoon leaders with the 173rd Airborne Brigade. One of them, Dave Ugland, had been in both the Rocket Club and the Russian Club with Mike Brennan, and he had been one of the Firsties who taught me how to ski during my Yearling year. For Mike and me, his death was a personal blow. But the other man was Clair Thurston, special friend of Deme Clainos from the Math Club and the guy who got a weekend in New York with that crazy German play for Deme, Art Mosley, and me.

And now they were both dead.

At West Point, Ugland and Thurston had both been on the brainy side: out of 565 graduates in the class of 1964, Ugland was ranked eighty-ninth overall and had won the American Legion award for standing first in the class in chemistry, while Thurston was ranked twenty-second and had won the General Pershing award for coming first in the class in tactics, and the American Bar Association award for having earned the same top spot in law.

Based on their academic success, the army would have paid for graduate programs for both men at any university in the country, but both had sensed that war was coming in Vietnam. Because of that, the sense of responsibility and duty to the nation that they had acquired at West Point caused them both to choose infantry. They went to three weeks of parachute training in Airborne School and nine weeks of suffering and endurance training in Ranger School, then on to their desired duty with the 173rd Airborne Brigade based in Okinawa, Japan.

That unit's paratroopers were the elite of the elite, and that was one reason why they were the first army unit assigned to fight in Vietnam. When November 1965 rolled around, after the unit had been in Vietnam for six months, both men had seen considerable action. In one contact, Clair was on his chest firing when he was struck in the buttocks by hand grenade shrapnel. When he was later evacuated, he even joked about going to the hospital to recover but not to "lay on his ass." After a few weeks in the hospital, he returned to lead his platoon back into combat, which was where he wanted to be.

In one of his last letters to his parents, Dave Ugland had wondered why so many of their friends were feeling sorry for him being in Vietnam. "I get a kick out of these people who think I'm being a martyr or something," he said, "I'm glad I'm here." His last letter told them of his preparations for the search-and-destroy mission that would cost him his life.

The First Battalion, 503rd Infantry of the 173rd had begun operations in the dangerous "Iron Triangle" north of Saigon on November 5. Ugland was a platoon leader in A Company, while Clair Thurston filled the same role in B Company. On Monday, November 8, both A and B companies found themselves in the heart of a major conflict with what turned out to be the Viet Cong's Q-761 Regiment, which outnumbered the First of the 503rd by a factor of 4 or 5 to 1. And make no mistake: the Viet Cong force by then was not made up of a bunch of farmers carrying machetes; rather, they were well-trained, well-armed, and pitiless soldiers.

A Company was moving forward when a storm of enemy gunfire hit them, and Ugland's platoon was quickly pinned down. Dave spied the location of a Viet Cong machine gun position and, with yells and gestures, pointed it out to his men. Then he stood up alone and rushed toward the enemy while firing his rifle from the hip. Only seconds later, the Viet Cong position turned on him, and their return fire cut him down, killing him instantly.

Meanwhile, B Company was on A Company's right, and the enemy fire came in from their left flank. Very quickly, Thurston saw what was happening and told his company commander that he wanted to lead his platoon forward and to their right, where they planned to set up on a small hill, then turn and attack the enemy's position from its left rear. With his commanding officer's approval, Clair and his men crawled ahead some thirty meters.

When they had reached what Clair thought was a good position, he made sure his platoon arrayed itself on either side of him to face the enemy. Once they were all in place, he stood up, yelled the classic infantry leader's command of "Follow me!" and moved forward, firing and roaring with his men. After only a few steps, return fire from the enemy ripped through his chest and ended his life.

Both men saved many American lives that day and played a major role in defeating the enemy force. For their actions, Ugland was later awarded the Bronze Star with a "V" for valor, while Thurston was awarded the Distinguished Service Cross, second only to the Medal of Honor for personal courage displayed on the battlefield. And while American casualties were high, the First of the 503rd eventually managed to drive off the Q-761 Regiment, which left the bodies of 394 dead Viet Cong soldiers behind them on the battlefield.

Dave Ugland's family had him buried back home in Minnesota. For Clair Thurston, however, an army brat who had graduated first in his class from the American high school in Heidelberg, Germany, while his father was stationed there and whose family had moved every few years, there really was no such home base. For him, then, there was no better final resting place than in the cemetery at West Point.

On Saturday, November 13, while the bruise we felt from the deaths in Vietnam of these latest two men was still raw, we got some surprising news. Somebody's girlfriend brought up a copy of that day's *New York Post*, which was not an option for daily delivery to Cadets. In that unblessed-by-academy-authorities newspaper, an interview with South Vietnamese Premier Ky was reprinted from the London *Sunday Mirror*. When asked who his heroes were, Ky answered that he had only one hero, and that was Hitler.

Cadets were shocked, but at one of our goat raid meetings, Art Mosley was just furious.

"*Hitler*? And that's from the guy who runs the government of South Vietnam, where American blood and treasure are being freely spent every day! *Hitler*? What kind of mess have our politicians gotten us into now?"

Mike Brennan chimed right in.

"I'll tell you what, instead of sending our troops out to fight the Viet Cong, they ought to send that same company from the 101st we saw at Buckner to just drag Premier Ky out in the street and do to him what we would have done to Hitler: the man ought to be shot down like a rabid dog!"

And Deme Clainos couldn't leave it alone either.

"What kind of idiot ally have we got over there? 'I have only one hero, and that's Hitler.' Well, you can kiss my ass, you Nazi sympathizer!"

Ky later scrambled around and explained that Hitler was his hero only because he made the trains run on time, or something else that was similarly silly. But he had said it, and we did not just lightly dismiss his words: Nazi sympathizer indeed!

In just a few days, we had gone through a lot of emotional turmoil. Even so, we had big plans afoot and we would not be deterred from our immediate goal down in Maryland. Through Adam, we again asked Mr. Acton to take his two daughters over to SPNSS on Sunday afternoon, November 14, and try to see the Navy goat. They did so, but the telephone report Adam got that evening was very negative.

First they had to go through an outer gate, and since they had no military ID cards, they were escorted by a Marine guard for perhaps a mile through what seemed to them a military housing area. Then they came to a ten-foot Cyclone fence topped by barbed wire, and another gate guarded by two Marines. The Navy goat, they were told, was kept in a pen made up of the same Cyclone fence topped with barbed wire and attached to the rear of this second and innermost guard post.

The road itself was blocked by a massive barrier, but rather than moving that, the Marines told them to park their car. Then they escorted Mr. Acton and his two daughters around the enclosed brick guard post on foot to where they could see inside the goat pen. And sure enough, there was Billy XIV, his enormous horns painted Navy Blue and Gold.

Mr. Acton told his son that if he tried to break in and steal the goat, he was really afraid for him. It just didn't seem remotely possible, he said, and those Marines all carried ugly black .45 caliber automatic pistols on their hips. He was sure they were good with them, and it seemed clear that they were not about to fool around with any trespassers, however they might have gotten inside this most secure inner fence. He also noted that the gate into the goat cage was secured with an enormous padlock, and he just saw no way we might also somehow purloin the key to that lock. And we certainly wouldn't be able to climb over that fence into the goat pen, then somehow lift the goat back out.

This report from Adam's dad was, frankly, discouraging. But how had Alexander coped with the Gordian knot? As part of our earlier preparation, we had already secured a set of four-foot-long bolt cutters from the post engineers, bolt cutters that, we were told, could cut through any padlock out there.

Transportation was another issue, but one of our group had that covered too. Because most of us would buy new cars at graduation—e.g., 107 of the 579 graduates in our class bought brand-new Corvettes from nearby A&C Chevrolet—we had selected several classmates as a car committee to negotiate with local dealers for the best prices possible. And one of our co-conspirators, Bob Lowry, happened to be the head of that class car committee. Early on in our planning that fall, he told us he was sure that he could get us a car to use in our attempted heist. And as it turned out, he did.

We were all geared up for our raid when it was announced in the mess hall on Tuesday, November 17, that Clair Thurston's funeral would be held two days later, after class on Thursday in the West Point cemetery. That would be two days before we were to launch, and his would be the first burial at West Point of a man fallen in battle who had, only a few years earlier, marched in parades as one of us.

As his Cadet brothers, and particularly because he had given Art, Deme, and me that free German play fiasco weekend trip to New York, the three of us really felt that we had no choice. And we were far from alone, as droves of other Cadets attended his burial in our hallowed ground.

West Point's cemetery sits atop a high bluff overlooking the Hudson. It is, appropriately, a quiet and somber place, with rows of stone memorials shaded by hardwood trees marking the graves, some ornate, some plain, of many graduates. To the Great American Public, the bulk of these had been unexceptional men, while even the minor lights cast by others in their era had mostly faded from memory. But all of them, despite the passage of time, are still important to West Point and so to the nation.

Among their number are Sylvanus Thayer, the fifth super-intendent of West Point who established it institutionally in the early nineteenth century and is remembered as the father of the military academy; Civil War generals Wesley Merritt, George Sykes, John Buford, and George Armstrong Custer (a brash but triumphant Union Army leader long before he was killed at the Battle of the Little Big Horn); George Goethels, who built the Panama Canal. Now, Clair Thurston would join them. And in his selfless sacrifice of his own life, he was among the noblest of them all.

Ashes to ashes, dust to dust.

Standing silent in the wind that probed our overcoats with icy stilettos, we could not avoid wondering if this might be what lay ahead for us: killed in war and buried back at West Point—the ultimate homecoming. In November 1965, given the ever-growing U.S. commitment in Vietnam and our loom-ing graduation just six months away, it was clear that we would not elude this war. So would that be our fate as well, to die in combat like Clair Thurston?

Words of the Roman poet Horace seemed to be everywhere, printed on paper, engraved on headstones, carved into our very minds.

Dulce et decorum est pro patria mori: It is sweet and right to die for your country.

We shivered from more than just the wind.

While the cleric read the words, Clair's black-garbed family bowed together in grief as sorrowful West Pointers hovered helplessly nearby. Yes, he was young. But he was dutiful. He was honorable. He was patriotic. Our popularly elected government had told him to go to Vietnam and fight, and he did, never for a moment questioning the ethical or legal propriety of our army's presence there. Rather, through his actions he personified West Point—Duty, Honor, Country—by offering, and then giving, his life for America.

The inscription on the stone left at Thermopylae reads: "Stranger passing by, go and tell the Spartans that here we lie, obedient to their orders." We had all eagerly sought to come to West Point, though we had never even considered at the time that a West Point ring might one day mean bloody death in battle for us.

It was soul draining to witness the burial that day of another earnest young West Pointer, a man very much like us, whose offering of his life for our country had been accepted. Many other young officers serving in the Vietnam War would follow. The unanswerable question we all kept buried in our hearts was whether we would be counted among their number.

Ashes to ashes, dust to dust.

17

The Adventure Begins

Two days later, we put aside these emotional blows, screwed up our courage to the sticking point, and made our move. First came transportation, and true to his word, it took only a phone call from Bob Lowry to A&C Chevrolet to secure a fast "muscle" car for our use in whatever way we wanted.

Next was the issue of personal safety. Mike Brennan had spoken to Captain Slinky, the army veterinarian who kept four army mules in a barn up near Michie Stadium. If we did get into the pen with the goat, Mike told us, Slinky said it would probably not make any noise. But he also said that if it was not familiar with us, it might well attack us.

Attack us?

That didn't deter us, but two big problems remained: We planned to try this after midnight, and once there, we were confident we could cut through the padlock. But how would we get inside that inner fence in the first place? And once there, how could we distract the Marine guards while we got the goat?

We had no answers, but ignorance of facts that might later be discovered only excited us more. We finally decided that we would just go to Adam Acton's home in Pasadena, Maryland, meet with his father for the latest intel, and then go from there. Worst case, we would still be away from West Point for a weekend. And if our dreams of glory were to be snuffed out, well, we would find a way to rationalize it and still have fun. But that was a glum prospect on which we refused to dwell.

On Friday, November 19, the first six of our group left on what was then considered a "long" weekend available only to seniors. But the other two of us, Art Mosley and I, had long-standing academic commitments and so could not leave West Point before early afternoon on Saturday, November 20.

When we finally got to Adam's place that Saturday, it was nearly seven in the evening and fully dark. But when the eight of us met in Adam's living room, Art and I were stunned to find that most of the others were ready to give up. Mr. Acton was very negative and did his best to talk us out of even trying. There seemed no possible way to get in without serious personal danger, he said, and he was almost pleading with us.

"Okay, men, it was a great idea, but you really have reached the end. There's just no way for you to get inside that fence, and I don't want to see any of you get shot trying to. And that's what they will do, like I told you. The orders of the guards who see trespassers are 'shoot to kill,' everyone who lives around here knows that, and I just don't want any of you to run that risk."

But I had just come off the highway after a five-hour drive, and I just didn't buy that.

"Sir, with all due respect, we're not at war, and I just can't believe they have blank orders to 'shoot to kill' any trespassers."

But Mr. Acton had a ready response:

"Okay, I don't want you men to be distracted here by what their orders might or might not be. But I wouldn't be surprised at all if they were told to shoot first and ask questions later."

Two of our group, Mike Brennan and Mike Mewhinney, had arranged for girls to meet them for the weekend, and these two had quickly become part of the group. Helen was Brennan's high school sweetheart. They were engaged to be married after graduation, and she had brought beautiful Juliana along as a blind date for Mewhinney.

As Mr. Acton spoke, there was a certain amount of nodding agreement around the room, some soft "mmm-hmms" that this was just too big a risk. But I wasn't about to abandon ship, so I stood up.

"Well, I don't care what their orders are, I'm not ready to throw in the towel before we even start. And remember, these are only Marines we have to worry about—we can outsmart them with our eyes closed."

Adam spoke up with a wide grin:

"Carhart, are you drunk?"

"No, I'm not drunk! And I want to run a recon, so who will go over there with me?"

Well, maybe I was a little bit high—I had probably had three or four cans of beer on the ride south—but I certainly was not drunk. Then Bob Lowry stood up with me.

"It's pretty easy to get there and I've got the car, so I'll show you."

Deme Clainos and Art Mosley also wanted to come, so the four of us jumped in the car, leaving our other four classmates and the two girls behind.

18

Recon Run

We made the ten-minute drive from the Acton home in Pasadena, Maryland, to the SPNSS, and as we approached the gate, I was suddenly very anxious. But Bob Lowry had already done this earlier that day, and as we approached the Marine guard at the gate, he just held his Cadet ID card out the window. We never really stopped, as the guard just glanced at it and waved us in, for Cadet ID cards were actually the same green plasticized cards as those carried by all active duty members of the U.S. military. With our short haircuts he probably just assumed we were fellow Marines and never took the time to look at the rank below the photo. That was a good thing, for it read "Cadet USMA" and that might well have given us away.

Once past the gate we were inside a military housing area, and we drove another half mile or so, passing a big parking lot in front of the post exchange, commissary, theater, and various other convenience outlets. Then we were in a wooded area, and a few hundred yards to our front was a brightly lit area for yet another gate, but this one blocked by a red-and-white-striped barrier of some sort, beside which was a brick guardhouse. As we got closer, a uniformed Marine came out of the hut and was obviously ready to stop us and ask to see our passes. But we had no such passes. Luckily, another road entered ours from the left, and Deme urged Bob to avoid the gate.

"Turn left, Bob, turn left!"

He did so, and looking back at the inner gate, we could just make out the fence of the pen behind the guardhouse in which the Navy goat was supposedly kept. As we drove, we found ourselves on a road that paralleled the barbed-wire-topped ten-foot Cyclone fence that walled off this part of the SPNSS. The hundred feet or so to our right between us and the fence was closely clipped grass, all brightly lit by floodlights. On our left were trees, but that soon opened into an area of townhouses and apartments.

We were moving slowly now, still wondering how we were going to get through that inner fence. Then, up ahead on our right was a pedestrian gate with another small guardhouse that covered it inside the fence. And despite the brightly lit area long the fence, this little hut was dark and obviously closed. A sidewalk led from that gate to the road on which we were driving, then continued on the other side along a road that led to the housing area.

Aha! So this was a pedestrian gate that must be used by personnel who lived in the housing area but worked inside the inner sanctum, this to save them having to drive. But it was Saturday night and it seemed there was not much work going on inside, for the gate was closed and the guardhouse was dark. Even so, a large sign was attached to the fence next to the gate, and it read:

Department of the Navy Property
Authorized Personnel Only
No Trespassing
Violators Will Be Prosecuted to the Full Extent of the Law

As Bob stopped and parked, we could see that the gate was secured by a padlock no bigger than the kind you would see on a high school locker. I went around back and got the bolt cutters out of the trunk while Lowry, Clainos, and Mosley walked up to the gate itself. When I got to them, Clainos stopped me with his arm and a stage whisper.

"No, no, we don't even need bolt cutters! Look!"

He had pulled down on the padlock and it simply popped open in his hand, showing that it had either been intentionally left unsecured or was simply broken. Then as I watched he lifted the lock, and it readily slipped up and out of the hasp. We all held our breath as he pulled back the now-unimpeded hasp and then pushed the gate, which swung open a few feet. The four of us froze, but there was no alarm, no bells, no clicking noise, no nothing!

We were all drop-jaw amazed: can it be this simple? Apparently, someone who lived in the housing area either had left the padlock unsecured so as to easily get to their work station over the weekend without having to drive through the main gate, or the padlock itself was defective. Either way, how convenient for us!

Deme pushed the gate open all the way, and still, so far as we knew, nothing unusual happened. I dropped the bolt cutters in the grass and the four of us quickly moved through the gate and out of the bright light, then slipped behind a cluster of dark and silent one-story buildings to our right. Pretty soon, we came to an open grassy field on an incline. Were we really inside the fence far enough to approach the main gate with the goat pen from the rear?

We weren't yet sure, so we raced up the slope in front of us. After a few hundred yards or so, we came to a clump of trees along the crest. Once through them, we could see a bright cluster of lights off to the right, with a road that ran toward it from below us on our left. As we watched, sure enough, we saw a car stop at the gate, then come through it and drive in our direction. And behind the guard post, we could see the faint outline of the goat pen.

That was enough evidence for us. Now stealing the goat would only require distracting the two Marines while we slipped up, broke the padlock, secured the goat, and took him back through the unsecured pedestrian gate. Suddenly, it sounded very simple indeed!

19

Decision Time

We raced back to the Acton house, by then so excited we could barely talk. Our energy was contagious, and within a few minutes of discussion, two of the other four Cadets in our group, Mike Mewhinney and Mike Brennan, joined us. But the remaining two, Adam Acton and Bill Blake, had given in to Mr. Acton's fears and decided to opt out of the raid. Adam was particularly outspoken.

"Now that you know you can get inside the fence, that just makes the whole thing even more dangerous, and you guys are going to end up getting shot and maybe killed! If you really try to pull this off, you guys are just plain crazy!"

But the six of us became even more confident as Adam talked. Hell, anyone can do the easy stuff! Now it was down to six of us, but we also had two beautiful young women who were not, like us, bound by the Cadet Honor Code and could therefore lie through their teeth to the Marine guards with complete impunity. But Mr. Acton wasn't through.

"Come on now, boys. Mike, you and Helen told me last night that you are engaged and plan to marry right after graduation next June. And the other Mike, I know you and Juliana are just a blind date, but you never know where that might lead. Why would you take a chance on really messing up a lovely romantic weekend in Maryland with some impossible fantasy? Why don't you guys just stop bickering and go out to have some beers. Adam knows a great place near here where a lot of college girls go, I'm sure the six of you can find dates there and have a lot of fun."

Mike Brennan answered.

"Mister Acton, no offense, but we're excited again, because that recon run group seems to have found a way for us to carry this off. And I know Helen supports me completely in this. In fact, she will play a key role in the whole plan, won't you, honey?"

Helen was not shy at all.

"You bet, and Juliana and I are completely in on this."

That seemed finally to quiet Mr. Acton, and very quickly our plan became for the six of us to drive back to the housing area around 11:30 p.m. Bob would turn left at the pedestrian gate and drive down the side road until he was close to the housing area. Then he would turn off the lights but keep the car running. The other five of us would move through the gate, then make our way to the trees from which we had seen the guard post. Once there, we would hide and wait.

We presumed that any change of the guard would take place at midnight, so we avoided that time. But at 12:25 a.m., or 0025 hours, Helen and Janet would drive up to the gate. They were hoping, they would tell the Marines, to find the Naval Academy, where they supposedly had blind dates waiting for them, but they somehow got lost.

We counted on their beauty and the not so subtle hints of sensuality they displayed overcoming whatever resistance might have remained in those poor Marines far from home in a lonely guard shack on a cold November night.

But though his father was through arguing, Adam Acton had taken on his cause.

"You guys are crazy! Just because you found a way through the fence does not mean you can just walk up and break into that pen and not get caught, or, hell, get shot! You seem to forget that these guys are well armed!"

Mosley spoke up.

"Come on, we're not at war, and even if they do see us, they're not going to shoot us."

Now Billy Blake spoke up, trying to get through to us.

"Guys, I think Adam and his father are right. This has been a great adventure so far, but I don't want to see this whole thing heading south and any of us getting seriously hurt, let alone arrested and thrown in jail, or even shot dead! The Supe specifically said we were not to go anywhere near this place, and if we get caught I think we might all get kicked out."

Lowry spoke up.

"Come on, Billy! They won't hear us or see us, they will be dazzled by Helen and Juliana."

But Blake wasn't through.

"Well, this time I think you're wrong, and you have already gone too far with you guys breaking through that pedestrian gate. Didn't you see those 'No Trespassing' signs Mr. Acton told us about?"

Clainos's response was quick.

"Yeah, we saw signs that said 'No Trespassing' and 'Violators Will Be Prosecuted to the Full Extent of the Law.' So what? We're not Russian spies or anything, and that's who the signs are for. We're just Cadets trying to steal the goat, that's all."

Then Mosley chimed in.

"We didn't break through anything, like I just told you. The padlock was not locked, we just lifted it out and pushed the gate open!"

But Billy was adamant:

"Yeah, well, I don't remember the specific details of 'breaking and entering' from our law course last year, but the gate was closed and the padlock was in place, so I think that's enough to make any trespasser guilty."

Adam spoke up again:

"I'm sorry, guys, but I agree with Billy and my father. I think if you go through that gate the way you propose, you will be in big trouble, not just with West Point but with the law. I vote against us going. I think we should just pack it in and I'll take you to Flanigan's Bar—there are always hot girls there from St. John's College, and we can have some real fun."

Billy also voted against launching this venture, but the other six of us supported the raid, as did the two girls. By then it was near 11:00 p.m., so while Billy and Adam stayed behind in the Acton house, the other six of us went out to Bob's muscle car and the two girls prepared to get in theirs, a station wagon Helen had borrowed from a friend. But before we left, Brennan called everyone together.

"Okay, guys, here we go. This is very high risk, but nothing ventured, nothing gained. Two guys have dropped out and it's down to us, so let's all put our hands together on this."

Mike extended his right hand and seven others joined his, two of them soft and delicate.

"All for one and one for all."

Silly words, perhaps, but we repeated them. Then we climbed into the two cars and chased our short-term destiny.

20

In Flight

This time, it was another car entering the security station whose headlights had shone on us, and we lay frozen for the brief eternity it took the driver to get around the girls and their car, then show his pass. We heard the barrier grinding open, then a dark car roared by us, the driver clearly ignoring whatever was inside the goat pen.

As we stood back up again, Mike pulled on Billy XIV's foot, and, surprisingly, it lifted readily. Then the rope was clear and the loop was soon over both horns and around his neck. Deme and Mike waved, and, as the last guy in, I opened the gate and started back the way we had come.

We had been a bit anxious about how the goat would react to our trying to lead him with ropes around his neck. But as he was led out the gate and turned right, moving away from the rear of the guard post, the goat started to run. The five of us had trouble keeping up with him, and I was out in front with Mosley, followed by Brennan and Clainos with the goat, and Mewhinney brought up the rear. And as our trail guy, before we left the goat cage behind, Mike did the very smart thing of picking up the broken padlock, closing the gate into the pen, and replacing the padlock through the hasp so that it looked completely undisturbed. Before he ran after us, he noticed the two Marines still entranced by the girls and completely unaware of what had just happened no more than twenty or thirty feet behind them. And because of Mike's care in reclosing the cage door and replacing the lock, they wouldn't discover that the goat was gone until long after the sun came up.

When Mewhinney caught up, we were five dark men running through the black in front of, beside, and behind that big white goat with the enormous blue and gold horns. And to our surprise, the goat was on our side, apparently thinking we were just Middies taking him out to some nighttime pep rally or something. He was more than eager to play, pulling Mike and Deme by the ropes around his neck as they raced along on either side of him. The grass below our feet was trimly mowed and the dark buildings and trees were so many blurs as we ran.

Before we came to the pedestrian gate, Art had raced ahead and opened it so that we barely even slowed down as we passed through. Again, Mewhinney, bringing up the rear, closed it behind us and replaced the open padlock. And now we were outside the enormous fence with the goat, who still pulled Mike and Deme along. A feeling of elation pumped through us all, but we still tried to make very little noise as we ran because we weren't completely out of the woods yet: we still had to go through one more gate before we were back in civilian Maryland where the U.S. Marines would no longer have the power to stop us.

Our run was now slightly downhill over more close-cropped grass, and a hundred yards ahead we saw the tail lights come on in our getaway car. The engine was loud as it strained toward us in reverse, then stopped. We opened the back doors and Clainos and Brennan piled in with the goat while Art and I jammed into the front seat beside Bob Lowry. There were no seatbelts in those days, and as soon as the back door slammed shut we were ready to go, but Brennan's shout stopped Lowry:

"No, no, wait for Mewhinney!"

Mike came running up behind the car with the bolt cutters in one hand. He threw them in the trunk, then jammed his body into the back seat beside Brennan, Clainos, and the goat. Then we were moving at high speed through the housing area.

"Carhart, you couldn't remember where you left the bolt cutters, but I found them."

"Where were they?"

"They were just laying in the grass by that last gate, and when I was looping the padlock back in place I saw those big brass balls in the grass shining up at me, and then I saw they were the ones on the end of the bolt cutters' black arms, so I grabbed them."

The blood drained from my face.

"Holy shit! Yeah, on our recon run I just put them down when we found the padlock was open and then I forgot about them. Thanks for saving my ass, Mike."

"Well, I don't think they're worth much, but they are painted with 'U.S. Corps of Engineers West Point,' and there's no sense leaving any evidence behind."

After a few turns, Bob slowed to a more cautious speed—no sense attracting attention in the dead of night on the grounds of the enemy. But inside the car, our excitement was electric. We were trying to get away before the two guards, temporarily distracted by the pretty girls, discovered the goat's absence, which would have resulted in an immediate closing of all gates. Mewhinney's replacing the locks would probably give us some time, so while suppressing our absolute joy—no, rapture!—Bob tried to move along like any family in their car would have done.

It was roughly half an hour or so after midnight, Saturday night/Sunday morning, there was no other traffic on the roads, but we still had to get past one last gate guarded by Marines before we were free. At that moment, we felt like characters in one of those John LeCarre spy movies where the star has to get past the guards, through the gate, and back into West Berlin without getting stopped or shot. We were that anxious, our breathing high and tight as we grew ever closer to the guard post.

In an effort to hide him, Brennan had tried to throw the black towel over the goat's head and horns. But that upset him and he started to lurch around, the horns suddenly a menace in tight quarters. He was bigger and heavier than any of the other back seat passengers, and the tips of his horns slashed through the fabric in the roof of this borrowed car. And more than that, the car was suddenly filled with a foul, acrid stench, for in his sudden fear, Billy XIV had just peed and shit all over himself. And all over Clainos, Brennan, and Mewhinney, who were smashed up next to him in the tight quarters of the rear seat.

This was too much, and windows were rolled down as we coughed and gagged. But we never stopped, for we were not yet off post and knew we could still be seized by the Marines and thrown into the slammer. Then we saw the gate directly in front of us, no more than a few hundred yards away. All the windows went back up, and as we approached we were simply terrified that nothing concealed those enormous blue and gold horns on a white goat jammed into the back seat with three grown men. Once we pulled into the lit-up area of the guard post protecting our only exit to freedom, any guard looking into our car would see the goat and would, no doubt, stop us. So coaching from the passengers was loud and insistent:

"If he tries to stop you, Bob, just pretend you don't see him and keep going!"

"Don't stop, Bob, don't stop!"

"Go! Go! Go! Go!"

We slowed to what seemed like almost a stop, and the six of us just stopped breathing. But the out-bound gate was wide open, and the bored Marine guard who was pulling watch for the graveyard shift just waved us through without really looking at us. To him, we were just another car full of men, ho-hum. And absent some alert call, he wasn't about to stop us.

Once past the guard, we all exhaled as Bob stepped on the gas. And as we turned onto a civilian highway, our glee erupted in hoots and cries of joy. But that, too, scared the goat and started him jumping and plunging, his immense horns banging Cadet heads while ripping and tearing more of the cloth roof liner. And it also brought on more peeing and shitting all over Brennan, Clainos, Mewhinney, and the back seat.

But Bob wasn't about to stop for something we could wash off later, so we quieted ourselves enough to calm the goat, somehow suppressing the spectacular streams of sunshine soaring through our senses. Lowry was the only sober mind in the car, and he carefully made the turns that got us back to the Acton house.

21

Hallelujah!

We soon pulled into the driveway and saw lights come on inside the house, then on the porch. Mr. Acton came out as Art Mosley stepped out of the front passenger's door and asked him to turn off the outdoor light. Once he had done so, we opened the back door and Billy XIV jumped out and shook his magnificent blue and gold horns.

Brennan and Clainos still held tightly to the ropes around his neck, but he made no effort to pull away and was just as calm as could be. Adam Acton and Billy Blake came out onto the porch, dumbfounded. Then Mr. Acton's two high school daughters and three of their girlfriends spilled out of the Acton house in wide-eyed wonder.

To these young girls, West Point Cadets, like older brother Adam, were very cool. When they had learned earlier that evening that we were going to try to steal the Navy goat, they never believed it possible for a moment. That was at the Severna Park Naval Security Station, where they had gone with their father and had seen the Navy goat inside a big cage with armed Marine guards all around—no one could get in there, let alone get back out—that simply wasn't possible! So to them, the sudden appearance of that very same Navy goat in their front yard with those same West Point Cadets who had just carried out their mission by stealing him from their Marine guards, why that was—it was just startling! Who are those guys?

This was a time of very rudimentary camera capability, but someone found a Brownie camera and took snapshots of the six of us with the goat. While we were posing, Helen and Juliana arrived, and once again, wild celebration was loose in the land, our shouts and laughter echoing down the block. There was a hose out back, and Brennan, Clainos, and Mewhinney were soon able to clean the crap off their clothes, though they now had wet pants legs for the long ride back to New York still in front of us. But our elation was such that they really didn't care at all.

Then Mr. Acton herded us all inside, and after we had calmed ourselves a bit, he sat down with us in his living room while his wife fixed us sandwiches for the long ride ahead of us.

"Okay, I will admit that I was wrong, and you are all to be congratulated. But do you realize what you just pulled off?"

We all shouted at once, followed by waves of laughter and heavy back pounding.

"We stole the Navy goat!"

He tried, with mixed success, to calm us down.

"Yes, yes, I know. But that's not what I mean."

We were dumbfounded. What else could there be?

"Listen, there's a much bigger story here. Do any of you know the story of Jason and the Golden Fleece?"

We had all heard of it more or less, and we had done something similar, but so what?

"Well, let me tell you about it. Long ago, I was a classics major in college, and 'Jason and the Golden Fleece' is one of the oldest Greek myths. It took place way before the Trojan War. Do you want to hear it?"

We again nodded while awaiting our promised sandwiches, not sure where this was going.

"Well, it seems that Jason was the son of a Greek king, but his uncle killed his father and took the throne. He tried to kill Jason, but his mother got away with him. Many years later, as a young man, Jason came back and tried to claim the throne.

His uncle grudgingly admitted Jason was right, but first sent him off on a mission to prove his worthiness.

"That mission was to go and find the Golden Fleece and bring it back, the sacred skin of an enchanted ram hidden and jealously guarded by another Greek king far away. The uncle thought his nephew would be killed in the effort, but Jason agreed to take it on. Then Jason recruited a band of Greek heroes to go with him and they set sail on a ship called the *Argus*, and became known as the Argonauts. You guys heard of that?"

We had, although only vaguely.

"Okay. Well, Jason found the right king, and he agreed to give the Golden Fleece to Jason, but only after he had performed some seemingly impossible tasks. That was going to take a while, so Jason and the Argonauts moved into the castle. After a while, Jason got to know the king's daughter, Medea, and the two fell in love and got engaged. Medea was also a sorceress, and she helped the Argonauts perform all these tasks.

"But her father still wouldn't give in, so she took Jason and the Argonauts to the cave where the Golden Fleece was hidden. It was protected by a dragon that never slept, but Medea enchanted him and kept him distracted while Jason and the Argonauts snatched the Golden Fleece. After that, Jason and the Argonauts took Medea with them, Jason married her, and they all got away on the *Argus* with the Golden Fleece. So do you see the connections?"

Mosley's brash voice split the silence.

"Yeah, but we stole the goat from a bunch of sailors and stupid Marines! And they are the ones who sail around on silly boats, so that sort of turns the tables on 'em, doesn't it?"

This was met with gales of laughter, but Mr. Acton held up his hand.

"You're right, maybe so. But from the cultural and mythological perspective, as young men you guys have shown yourselves to be modern-day Argonauts. And Mike Mewhinney and Juliana, I know this is just your first date, but Mike Brennan and Helen, you two are engaged to be married, correct?"

Brennan's response was immediate and booming.

"Ab-so-lute-ly!"

We all laughed, but Mr. Acton was right on it.

"Okay, then, there it is, as plain as the nose on your face. Mike, you are modern-day Jason, and Helen, you are Medea who distracted the never-sleeping dragon U.S. Marine guards while the rest of you Argonauts stole the Golden Fleece! What could be clearer?"

The laughter that followed became whoops of glee, with much hugging and back-pounding. What, indeed, could be clearer?

22

Caravan Crisis

As we began to plan our return to West Point, we suddenly realized that driving the goat would be problematic. While we met inside, two of the high school girls had been walking the goat in the Acton's backyard while the three others did their best to clean the goat leavings out of the back seat of Bob's car. But it still stank, and we could expect more from Billy. This was a problem, so we decided that two of us would ride with the goat in the getaway car. These "goat guards" would endure the stench as best they could, while the others would ride with Helen Brennan in her borrowed station wagon.

And so it was that we set off in a two-car convoy, headed north and home to West Point where, in the eyes of the rest of the Corps of Cadets, we would be received as heroes. We would not, however, be so perceived by the superintendent, but we would figure out how to handle that later. At the moment, we had to take the Golden Fleece back to West Point with us.

I was the only one who knew how to get to my grandmother's farm, so Art Mosley and I took the first tour of duty driving the goat car. And as we drove, Art and I were as high as we had been hours earlier in the aftermath of what could only be described as a Cadet triumph. The car windows were closed on that frigid late-November night, and the air we breathed was just putrid. But at that point, we could have endured almost anything.

At the end of our ride would be my grandmother's farm in

Eagle Mills, New York, a small farming village outside of Troy and perhaps two hours north of West Point. We planned to park Billy there, then return to West Point, get the word of our success out to the Corps of Cadets, and just roll with the punches.

We got some disbelieving looks from the bridge toll-takers in Maryland and Delaware—two men with black-smeared faces, a huge white goat with massive blue-and gold-painted horns in the back seat of a hot muscle car—what were we, part of a circus? Our barely concealed joy at their confusion was a reflection of what we had just done.

Yes, this could be described as a sophomoric college prank. But those U.S. Marines in the Shore Patrol guarding the main gate into the Severna Park Naval Security Station carried loaded pistols on their hips, and we believed that, had they seen us, they might have shot first and asked questions later. So our overflowing glee was tempered to a certain extent by the relief of having gotten away, not only with no shots having been fired, but also without us ever having been detected at all!

Near the northern end of the New Jersey Turnpike, we pulled into a rest stop and changed goat guards. The getaway car once again took the lead, and as I slipped into the back seat of Helen's station wagon, I never even considered what might happen if the car I was in lost contact with the goat car.

Bad decision.

The new goat guards immediately screwed up their faces in disgust as they tried to adapt to the stench, then our two-car convoy started north on the New York Thruway. We had maybe two hours in front of us to the Troy exit we needed, after which we would follow my directions to Eagle Mills. I gratefully laid my head against the door pillar and within seconds was deep asleep.

Suddenly I was startled back to life by a loud metallic grinding noise. It was just after dawn, and as our suddenly dead-engine car pulled to the side of the New York Thruway, the driver leaned frantically on the horn, trying to signal the goat getaway car in front of us that we had lost all power. But the horn-blowing and headlight-flashing was to no avail as the driver of that car, Deme Clainos, was also dead tired. Consequently, he never heard our horn or saw our lights and just kept going, oblivious to our breakdown.

This was well before cell phones, of course. But even if we had located a dial-up pay phone at a gas station, say, there was simply no way for us to contact the driver of the goat car. This was a big problem because, beyond heading north on the New York Thruway, neither Deme nor his fellow passenger/goat guard, Mike Brennan, had any idea of where to go. So what were we to do now?

Being able to think creatively and remain flexible as conditions and situations changed was one of the hallmarks of successful military mission performance, just the sort of thing we had been drinking in at West Point for three and a half years. Sometimes the drinking had been as if from a fire hose, such as during Recondo training at Camp Buckner. But by this stage in our professional development we were readily able to think on our feet and keep the effort going, whatever the unforeseen barriers that might suddenly erupt in our faces and possibly foil our carefully laid plans.

As it happened, the blown engine occurred when we were just past the exit for Central Valley, which was ten or fifteen miles west of West Point. We quickly decided that Art and I would walk across a couple of pastures to a back road that headed east. Things were a bit more complicated because this was just after dawn on a Sunday morning, and there was not a lot of traffic on the roads.

Luckily, Art and I were able to catch a ride with a man headed that way, and by 8:00 a.m. we were slipping back into Cadet barracks in Central Area where we both lived. We were wearing Levis and dark turtlenecks, our faces blackened by burnt cork for the operation, and we got some funny looks from Plebes who were delivering newspapers.

Chapel formations had already marched off, and we immediately started walking through the barracks, looking for someone who had access to a car. That didn't take long because John Ford, another classmate in E-2, had a girlfriend staying at the Thayer Hotel, and she had a car. Within a half hour we were headed back north on the New York Thruway.

We soon came to the broken-down station wagon, still sitting on the side of the road where we had left it. They had already been visited by the New York Highway Patrol, and a tow truck was on its way. Helen and Janet urged us to try to catch up with the goat car, assuring us they would be okay and would try to meet us that afternoon back at West Point. So Bob Lowry and Mike Mewhinney got into the car with me, Art Mosley, and John Ford.

Within about ten miles we came to a rest stop, and as we pulled into it we immediately saw Mike Brennan and Deme Clainos standing off the edge of the parking lot with the goat, who, with two slack ropes around his neck held by our classmates, was quietly grazing.

We got to my grandmother's soon enough, and my uncle put the goat in a clean stall in his big dairy barn. Clainos had a camera, and he took a picture of the other five of us, which ended up in our West Point class yearbook. Then we made our way back to West Point.

23

Laying Low

Sunday evening, I used our only immediate access to the outside world, a pay phone in the barracks basement, to call one of the big radio networks in New York City. After I said that we, a group of West Point Cadets, had stolen the Navy goat, I was put through to a well-known sports announcer named Mel Allen. Other Cadets were walking by the pay phone, and we were not yet ready to tell the Corps of Cadets what we had done, so in hushed tones I described to Allen what we had done, finishing by saying the Navy goat was being kept in a secure location for the time being, but that we expected to present it to the captain of the Army football team at a ceremony of sorts later in the week.

Mel Allen loved the story, which he tape-recorded and told me he would play the next morning on his sports talk show. And sure enough, early that Monday morning the story was loose on the wires. Since I had been speaking on the phone in little more than a whisper, no one at West Point could really recognize my voice. Some thought it a made-up story, but down in Washington DC, the senior admiral responsible for the entire navy was the chief of naval operations (CNO), Adm. David L. McDonald. And he, we heard, was livid with rage.

Like virtually all four-star navy admirals, McDonald was himself a graduate of the Naval Academy. And his fury erupted primarily because some unknown persons had been able to penetrate the highest-security installation in the U.S. Navy, spirit away the almost-sacred possession of the Naval Academy, and remain undetected for many hours.

We learned this because one of Admiral McDonald's Naval Academy classmates and close friends from their Annapolis days together was another admiral, whose youngest son was none other than Mike Mewhinney.

Mike's father, Leonard S. "Tex" Mewhinney, had retired from the navy when Mike was in his teens and became a college professor at North Texas State. Mike also had a younger brother who was then a midshipman at the U.S. Naval Academy, and he had told neither of them about our goat theft plot before we pulled it off. But that Sunday night, his father called Mike.

The CNO, Admiral McDonald, knew his Naval Academy buddy Tex Mewhinney had a son who was a West Point Cadet. So McDonald had asked him, "off the record," to try to find out through his son if it was indeed West Point Cadets who had done this. If so, there were no other security concerns. But if not, then it looked like the goat theft might be part of some elaborate ruse, a distraction from something else going on inside the SPNSS. Something else that could only be bad for the U.S. Navy.

So what do you say when your father, a Naval Academy graduate and retired admiral, asks you point-blank if you know anything about the missing goat? Mike first pleaded with his father not to use any names. But then he told him everything, and Mike could hear his father chuckling quietly as he listened.

He agreed that no names would be mentioned for now, but that he would tell the CNO in general terms that he knew for certain that West Point Cadets had indeed done this deed, and the goat was still alive and safe on a farm somewhere in New York. But if this matter ever became public, he said, he would make sure that McDonald read the Mewhinney name on the list of six West Point Cadets who had so publicly thumbed their noses at the navy.

Before Taps Sunday evening, we had all heard Mike's story about the CNO, and we were simply delighted! And on Monday morning, the Corps of Cadets was abuzz with the news about the theft of the Navy goat that they had heard on the radio. So whose voice was that hoarsely whispering and claiming to be a Cadet? Many Cadets thought it was just some elaborate hoax, while others believed it. But if it was not a Cadet, who in their right mind would pretend to be one just to cause such a ruckus over nothing?

When we were at breakfast in the mess hall Monday morning, there had been brief articles in the *New York Times* sports pages as well as in other papers from around the country alluding to the supposed theft, though the Naval Academy simply had no comment on the matter. But as we knew from Mewhinney, the Naval Academy had not discovered Billy XIV was missing until mid-morning Sunday. So Mike's extra effort to close the goat pen door after we had left and loop the broken padlock back through the hasp seemed to have paid off, and that had surely helped us get back out through that second gate into the civilian world of Maryland so cleanly.

When we got to class, the instructors had either ignored the story completely or just brushed it off, saying that the whole story seemed preposterous. And to most of those who commented on it, there was simply no way any Cadets might have gone down to Annapolis and duped those naval officers and Marines charged with security at the highest-security installation of the U.S. Navy—it just couldn't be done, so they dismissed it as an elaborate rumor.

When class broke for "mid-period," from about 9:30 a.m. until 11:00, I went over to North Area to Deme Clainos's room. Like Art Mosley and Mike Brennan, Deme was a Cadet captain and a company commander. Bob Lowry was also a Cadet captain, but he was second regimental adjutant rather than a company commander, which meant that he wore somewhat fancier stripes on his sleeve.

Cadet captain was a rank only accorded to perhaps one out of every twenty men in the class, so our group was a somewhat illustrious one that included four Cadet captains. Mike Mewhinney was, like half the class, a Cadet lieutenant, while I was a lowly sergeant, perhaps the bottom 40 percent or so, according to the tactical department's appreciation of our individual "aptitude for the service." I really didn't care about Cadet rank, and it's true that I was a bit of a "Peck's bad boy," always getting in trouble for something or other. But in this enterprise I had high-ranking Cadets who were my comrades-in-arms and—bottom line—blood brothers.

We had intentionally kept quiet about the goat, and on Monday morning very few other Cadets even knew anything of the whole operation. We still planned to go get the goat in Eagle Mills later that week, bring him back to West Point, and somehow present him to the captain of the football team in front of the rest of the Corps of Cadets—maybe in the mess hall before dinner one day, but we had still not worked out those details. Now, however, we were hearing all sorts of wild conjecture from other Cadets and instructors, and that was counterproductive at best. So what were we to do?

Deme suggested that we write a blunt statement that we had the goat, saying that plans for his future appearance were being developed, and telling everyone to keep quiet about it. We would then print up copies and put them on every table in the mess hall before lunch. This, of course, was well before Xerox copy machines were invented. So while I knocked out the statement on Deme's company typewriter, he got on the dial-up phone (one of which company commanders had in their rooms) and tried to locate a mimeograph machine, which was the only way papers could be copied at the time.

He finally located one in the office of the West Point Band, in the back of the tangle of administrative buildings down below the Plain. It was still early and we had more than an hour before our 11:00 a.m. class, so Deme and I trotted down the hill. When we got there a senior sergeant was in charge. Deme, wearing his readily recognized Cadet rank on his shirt collar, spoke up.

"Good morning, Sergeant. I am Mister Clainos and I'm the company commander of Company K-2. I'm here with my classmate, Mister Carhart, because we have a bit of a problem. We have written a special message to the Corps of Cadets, and we want to make a few hundred copies so that we can put one on each table of the mess hall before dinner today. I have learned that you have a mimeograph machine, so I wonder if you would let us use it for a few minutes."

The sergeant was a bit perplexed.

"I don't know about that, Mister Clainos, we only use our mimeograph machine for sheet music, and the paper and ink are both expensive—we only get so much each month. Is this message any kind of official business?"

"No, it's not."

"Well then, I'm sorry, Mister Clainos, but I just do not have the authority to allow you to make copies on our machine. If I did and I got caught I would have to pay for the ink and paper myself and I would be in big trouble . . ."

Deme extended the typewritten message to him.

"Here, read this."

Last Saturday night a team of firsties went to a naval security station near Annapolis where the Navy goat is kept before the game. We got inside, then distracted marine guards with girls while we broke into his pen and stole the Navy goat. He is now on a farm in New York and will soon be presented to the football team. The Tactical Department is after us so if you know anything about this please don't talk.

The sergeant perused the words, then looked up, his face lit up by a wide smile. "We've been talking about this around the office. Apparently there was some Cadet on the radio this morning claiming that he and some others had stolen the Navy goat. So it's true?"

"As true as the sun comes up in the morning, Sergeant. And now that you know, I would ask you to just forget our names. So what do you say?"

The sergeant stood up, his hand and the message quivering.

"Absolutely! I never even saw your name tags, so come on, I'll show you how this machine works."

We had to literally crank out each copy by hand, and soon purple ink was running on the floor. The sergeant told us not to worry about that, but he only had enough paper to make 189 copies, which we laid out to dry on tables and desks and even the floor. Within a half hour or so, we had stacked our dried mimeographed papers into two cardboard boxes the sergeant gave us, and then we sprinted back up the hill.

A bit out of breath, we walked into the front of the mess hall, bold as brass, where the waiters were literally laying out plates and silverware. They gave us funny looks but we smiled back as we raced up and down the aisles, Deme in one wing of the mess hall and I in the other. We had to skip tables now and then, but we knew that, once the Corps came in and a message of this import to them personally was read, the news would spread like wildfire.

With the delivery of all 189 copies complete, Deme and I parted and I raced back to my room and picked up my books for my 11:00 class: History of the Military Art. I barely made it, but I always looked forward to this class.

Today we would discuss Napoleon at the 1805 Battle of Austerlitz, where he tricked the Russian and Austrian forces into dividing, then crashed between them and utterly crushed both armies. Ours was not such a resounding military success, of course. But even so, for a bunch of callow Cadets supposedly still learning the basics of military operations, we had pulled off quite a feat. And we had embarrassed the hell out of the U.S. Navy!

When we formed up to march to dinner, there was some initial buzz about the goat. But so far nothing had corroborated that supposed-Cadet's voice on the Mel Allen show earlier that morning, so skepticism had begun to set in. But within a few minutes of entering the mess hall, shouts of glee and laughter began ringing off the walls.

Wow! We really do have the Navy goat!

So far as I know, none of the six of us shared any further information with classmates. But now the word was out, and during that meal the Corps of Cadets was suddenly caught up in a celebratory mood. After the meal, however, we all had to go to various classes. But on the smiling faces of virtually all Cadets, the same wide-eyed message could be read:

Wow! Dreams really do come true! Wow!

24

Inside Connections

That afternoon, we began brainstorming for some way to get an inside line into how the West Point hierarchy was reacting to all of this. The four Cadet captains in our group were all reluctant to tell their tactical officers of their involvement because this whole affair was already ballooning out of control, and that just seemed too risky at this point. So what could we do?

As it happened, my Cadet company commander during our Beast Barracks and then later during our Plebe academic year was Tom Carney, who had graduated in 1963. In fact, when we went over the wall in civilian clothes the day before Christmas and brought back B-4 bags full of beer, I had taken some of Tom's civilian clothes out of his locker and worn them, including a pair of size 14 white buck shoes that flapped on my feet like swim fins.

But that was long ago. As it happened, however, Carney had been quite a star in the army. In the fall of 1965, as a first lieutenant, he had been named to the prestigious post of aide de camp to the commandant of Cadets, Brig. Gen. Richard P. Scott. I had seen him once or twice since then in Central Area, and although he did nothing more than wink and smile at me, it was still an acknowledgment that we had been in the same Cadet company only three years earlier, and he remembered me.

Because of this previous relationship, it was decided by the group that I should approach him and see if he would be willing to share any information he might have learned. Tuesday morning between classes, I went to the commandant's office and asked to meet with him. He called me into his office with a smile and pointed to a chair, where I sat.

"What's up, Tom? Are you one of the guys who stole the Navy goat?'

He said that almost as a throwaway line, for the academy was abuzz with conjecture.

"Sir, before we go any farther, may I ask that this conversation be held in confidence?"

Trick words, maybe, but we had learned in our law courses Cow year that if another officer agrees to speak or listen "in confidence," then he or she is at least honor bound, and maybe legally bound, not to reveal the contents of the conversation. Carney suddenly grew serious.

"Sure, Tom, this will be in confidence. But what's this about? Are you in trouble with a woman or something?"

"No, sir, it's nothing like that."

I lowered my voice and leaned forward.

"Sir, I know you weren't serious when you first asked me, but in fact I am one of the guys who stole the Navy goat."

Tom leaned forward on his desk, suddenly incredulous.

"What?"

"Yes, sir, I'm one of the guys who stole the Navy goat."

Tom stood up and closed his door, then returned to his desk.

"Where is it?"

"Sir, right now it's on my grandmother's farm in Eagle Mills, New York, about two hours north of here."

"Okay. Don't tell me any more. What do you need from me right now?"

"Sir, we don't need anything from you. However, I understand the authorities here are a little bit upset over this, and we just need a wire to the inside. That is, if any plans are made to take unusual steps to catch us, like calling in every Cadet and asking them on their honor if they know anything about the Navy goat, we'd sure like to know about it ahead of time."

"Don't worry, they're never going to use your honor against you, I don't think that's ever happened before. But Tom, because of my position I just can't get involved in this directly."

There was a painful pause, but as I stood up, Carney waved me back into my chair.

"Hold on, hold on. I think I know how we can handle this with few fingerprints, so stay here for a moment."

I slumped back in my chair, suddenly frightened. Was my old Cadet company commander going to turn me in? But after a few minutes the door opened and Carney came back in, followed by another man in uniform.

"Mister Carhart, this is Sergeant Major Bill Hall. He's the brigade sergeant major and he handles a lot of the commandant's work, so he's as close to the throne as I am."

Sergeant Major Hall's handshake was very strong.

"Mister Carhart, Lieutenant Carney tells me you are involved in a pretty important exercise."

Before I could answer, Carney spoke up.

"Mr. Carhart, you can trust the sergeant major completely. I told him what you told me, but this affair has the highest attention, not only here but also in the Pentagon. And so because of the interest this has generated at the highest levels, it would just be too dangerous for you to come to see me anymore. All of a sudden people are suspicious of everyone and everything. I won't reveal what you told me, but from now on, if I pick up any information that might be of use to you, I will pass it on to the sergeant major and he will pass it to you. Understand?"

"Yes, sir, and thank you."

"Okay, now, let's keep this low-key, so you two go to the sergeant major's office around the corner and continue your talk."

We stepped into the hallway and twenty feet away went into a smaller office, where the sergeant major sat down and gestured to a chair for me.

"So you guys really did get the Navy goat?"

"Yes, Sergeant Major, we did. Right now he's inside a barn

on my grandmother's farm in Eagle Mills, New York, about two hours north of here."

"Very interesting. I won't ask you right now how you did it, but once the smoke clears I'd love to hear the details."

I hesitated, and the sergeant major took a sheet of paper out of a desk drawer and handed it to me. It was one of the fliers we had put on tables in the mess hall telling other Cadets we had the goat.

"Do you know about this?"

"Yes, Sergeant Major, we wrote this and put it on tables in the mess hall."

"Well, you have to be careful all the time, even here. You may think that your classmates are all your trusted brothers, but it's no different here than anywhere else, 'cause there are always so-called trusted friends who would run over anyone, even their own mothers, just to get ahead. No fewer than three different Cadets, maybe more, delivered copies to the commandant's office yesterday afternoon, and probably more were turned in to company tactical officers. So be careful who you share secrets with."

I was not really surprised, but nodded my assent.

"Don't worry, Sergeant Major, very few people outside our group know anything."

"Good, keep it that way. I should tell you, however, that the Supe, General Lampert, is really pissed. He was over here raging around just a few hours ago. That's because you guys broke what was supposedly a gentlemen's agreement between the supes at Annapolis and West Point. The agreement was that neither Cadets nor midshipmen would mess with each other's mascots during the two weeks before the Army-Navy game, and he made sure that very threatening regulations to that effect were broadcast to the Corps."

"I know, Sergeant Major, we all knew. But it was not made an honor offense, so we just figured 'catch us if you can,' and so far they have not. And I hope they won't unless you or Lieutenant Carney turn us in."

"Well, you don't have to worry about that from either of us, Mister Carhart. The Supe still isn't convinced it was Cadets who did this—he thinks it's some elaborate prank that Mel Allen is pulling just to hype his show. But down in the Pentagon, the senior navy admiral, the chief of naval operations, well, we've been told that he is just furious."

I was a bit confused.

"Well, I would say I'm sorry, Sergeant Major, except that I'm not."

"Forget that, you're among friends here—at least inside my office. But this is a whole lot more than some college prank, which is what it might look like from the outside, so let me tell you what I know has happened. Yesterday morning, about ten o'clock, while you men were all in class, the Supe brought over a blistering message he got from the Naval Academy Supe about breaking his word and so on, and how some Cadets had apparently committed a federal crime of trespass at Severna Park. And he's furious."

Suddenly my blood ran cold."

"A federal crime?"

"That's what he said. And he made it clear that if it's Cadets who did this—and he still doesn't know for sure right now—he wants to catch them and, whoever they are, prosecute them under the law for criminal trespass or something, that wasn't clear to me. And he said that if they don't end up in jail for that, he would make sure that they are dismissed from the academy. That's what he told the Com yesterday afternoon, and Lieutenant Carney and I were standing right there listening to him."

I felt my heart fall through my stomach.

"What . . . what does the Com say?"

"Well, not much so far. He thinks we should just wait until we're sure it was Cadets and if it was he is really going to push hard to find out who they are. But let me get back to the story we heard from our Supe, who heard it from his contacts at the Naval Academy—which probably means our exchange tactical officer. But he is really mad and he started out by saying 'This is not funny,' so none of us laughed, at least not in front of him. Anyway, it seems that the Marine guards had a watch change in the early morning hours Sunday, but they didn't go in the pen and check on the goat, as they were supposed to. Apparently the padlock was still in place and I guess they just assumed he was asleep inside his little hootch, same thing he did every other night. Then a few hours later, some navy junior officer from the Naval Academy took his daughter over to Severna Park to see the Navy goat, and when the guards went to open the pen, they found the padlock was broken and the goat was gone. Now that was Sunday morning. Yesterday, Monday morning, most of us know about this sports news blast on the radio with someone claiming to be a Cadet, and that he was part of a group from the class of '66 that had gotten inside the wire of the Severna Park Naval Security Station, distracted the guards with girls, and climbed over the fence into the goat pen and took him away without the guards even knowing they were there. Is that true?"

"Well, we didn't climb over the fence, but basically, yes, it is, Sergeant Major."

"Here's what we have heard so far. At Severna Park, there's two layers of concentric fences, one inside the other, each with its own gate guarded around the clock by U.S. Marines, as you probably know by now . . ."

"Yes, Sergeant Major, but we got waved through the first gate with our Cadet ID cards."

"Okay, but for right now don't tell me anymore about how you did it. The navy is mad because you seem to have pulled off this raid without a hitch, and the Marines didn't even know you had been there until the next morning, so the navy security people are going ballistic and heads will surely roll."

I shrugged.

"Sergeant Major, like I said, I would apologize if I felt bad, but I don't."

"Nor should you, Mister Carhart. And heads *should* roll,

because you guys could have been spies and their security was lax, to say the least. So anyway, this got all the way up to the chief of naval operations, the senior admiral who runs the navy and who is himself an Annapolis grad, and he just went crazy. Not because you stole the Navy goat, mind you—well, there's probably a little bit of that mixed in—but mostly because whoever stole the Navy goat was able to get past their guards and fences and so on at their hotshot security station. That's where they have important research labs, lots of other classified stuff. And luckily these trespassers—I guess it was you men—only wanted the Navy goat that happened to be kept in a pen right behind the main guard post, which was supposedly all lit up during the night."

"I know, Sergeant Major, and you're right, it was as bright as daylight."

"But see, to them, you could just as easily have been Russian spies, and the Marines didn't discover the goat was gone until well into the morning hours. It was broad daylight and they never even thought to take a close look. So you guys pulled off something a lot bigger than you ever suspected."

Mewhinney's idea to close the gate after we had taken the goat and loop the broken padlock back in place had actually worked! Hallelujah!

"Well, Sergeant Major, we've already heard about the CNO's anger, but we're not spies, we just wanted the goat, that's all."

"I know, I know. But as you may suspect, there is a lot of pressure here right now to find out if it really was Cadets who stole it, and if so, who they are. The Supe is the one who is really death on this, so stay away from him."

"Oh, I will, don't worry about that. But if you or Lieutenant Carney find out something we should know, how will we contact each other?"

Hall stood up and went to a window that looked out on Central Area, through which most Cadets passed every day.

"Okay, I've got a little 'Beat Navy' sticker right here on the window sill. If I need to get info to you, I can always call your company, but that could be dangerous for you. So every morning and afternoon, when you are going to or from class, just look at the lower corner of this window. If the 'Beat Navy' sticker is taped to the window where you can see it, that means I want you to call me. My extension is 9757. Here, I'll write it down."

He handed me a small piece of notepad paper with the number.

"Anything else?"

I shrugged.

"Not for now, Sergeant Major. But thank you for taking a chance on us."

"Mister Carhart, it's the least I could do.

"Thank you, Sergeant Major."

"You're welcome, Mister Carhart. Now be careful who you share any of this information with, and don't trust anyone, even your classmates. Remember, the walls have ears."

My cheeks were afire and my heart soared as I walked out of the commandant's office building and across Central Area to my room. Suddenly, I felt like I was in a James Bond movie, and it felt great! But I also knew that I had to be careful and trust no one.

The next morning, Wednesday, there was no "Beat Navy" sticker in SGM Hall's window, nor was it there that afternoon. But the morning paper also reported that U.S. casualties in the Vietnam War for the preceding week were 240 killed in action and 470 wounded in action. Pretty sobering food for discussion over breakfast.

But then a pretty normal day of classroom tedium ensued. The casualty figures were not easily dismissed, but only put aside. For a while. Soon enough, these and similar numbers would be haunting reminders of what lay ahead for all of us.

Before dinner, I met with Art Mosley in his room, and he had just spent an hour in the office of a major who taught engineering. And Art was mad.

"You know I just spent time talking to one of my professors about a project I'm working on. And when we were through, he said that because I'm a Cadet company commander I should choose infantry."

"Okay, lots of them are pushing their branches. So what?"

"Well, it's not so much that he was pushing his own branch, but it was how he said it."

"Which was?"

"He had the gall to tell me I should go infantry because as a young lieutenant I would be able to go to Vietnam and get right in the thick of the fight. He said that way I could make a name for myself and it would be a great professional op-por-tun-i-ty for me! That's Op-por-tun-i-ty!"

"So what did you say?"

"Well, I told him 'No thank you, sir, I am going into the Corps of Engineers.' But I should have said, 'Op-por-tun-i-ty, my ass!' You're a major, so it's easy for you, majors are never in combat. And when you were a lieutenant, there was no war for you to go to. But as for me, you want me to go infantry, then go to Vietnam and see if maybe I can get killed and be remembered as a brief shining moment of glory by other West Pointers who did not get killed, sort of the way they have treated Clair Thurston!"

"Art, you're really pissed, aren't you?"

"You're damned right I am! 'Op-por-tun-i-ty,' my ass! And after what Premier Ky said about Hitler being his hero, I think we should just tell them to fight their own fight and leave us out of it! We have no business trying to prop up a bunch of tin pot dictators!"

I managed to calm Art down by changing the subject. We talked about bringing the goat back to West Point, and Art thought we should tell someone on the football team who we are. So I told him what Sergeant Major Hall had told me about classmates of ours giving copies of those fliers we made to the Com's office, and he agreed that we should just keep quiet. But what do we do about the goat?

I had met with Lieutenant Carney and Sergeant Major Hall that morning, and there was no "Beat Navy" sticker in Hall's window that evening before supper. There had been brief articles in the Tuesday sports pages of both the *New York Times* and the *Herald Tribune* that had only sketchy details. The Naval Academy had acknowledged that the Navy goat was missing, but they said they were certain that West Point Cadets were not behind the abduction. The superintendent's office at West Point also said that no West Point Cadets were involved, but other than that, they had no information on the matter.

25

Time to Deliver

On Wednesday morning, coming back from class at mid-period around 9:45, I saw the sticker in Sergeant Major Hall's office. I didn't want to make such a phone call in the company orderly room, the only location where a phone available for Cadet use could be found, so I went directly to Art Mosley's room. As Cadet company commander, he was the only Cadet in our company who had a phone in his room. He wasn't there when I walked in, so I just picked up the phone and dialed 7897.

"Sergeant Major Hall, sir."

"Hello, Sergeant Major, this is Mister Carhart. I just came out of class and I saw the 'Beat Navy' sticker in your window."

"Good. Just a minute, let me close my door."

I heard some shuffling, then Hall was back on the line, but this time, his voice was hushed.

"Now listen carefully, Mister Carhart. I don't know what you are going to do with this information, but Lieutenant Carney and I both agreed that you and your friends need to hear it. The Supe was over here again today, and he was just in a fury. He only stayed a few minutes and he went into General Scott's office and closed the door behind him. Now General Lampert is ordinarily a very reserved man who does not anger easily. But you could hear him yelling at General Scott all the way down the hall. He had no more than walked out the door when General Scott sent for all four army colonels who are the regimental commanders, and three of them were here within minutes. Colonel Hamblen is at the Pentagon, but his deputy came. And now the plan is—and this comes from the Com, but the Supe is clearly behind it—that probably starting tonight, officers from the Tactical Department are going to go to the rooms of every Cadet who went on weekend leave and confront them with a blunt question: 'Yes or no, do you know anything about the missing Navy goat?'"

I felt my heart sink.

"Wow. So they are going to use our honor against us?"

"Mister Carhart, that's not the worst of it, because we could hear part of what the Supe was yelling at General Scott. We know he said that if Cadets were involved, that meant they had violated his specific orders not to go anywhere near the Naval Academy and so they had embarrassed not only him and West Point, but the whole United States Army. He said that if he found out Cadets were involved, he would see that they are prosecuted for intruding into a highly restricted area and if they don't end up in jail for that he would make sure they are dismissed from the academy."

Now my heart really did sink.

"Sergeant Major, did you say 'dismissed'?"

"That's right, Mister Carhart, that's what he said."

"But Sergeant Major, how can he throw us out? We didn't break the honor code or anything, those were just regulations, so how can he kick us out?"

"Mister Carhart, you have to realize, the Supe's under a lot of pressure over this, he probably just got off the phone with some other general in the Pentagon, and he's been embarrassed. Now you may have technically trespassed in doing this, but as a practical matter, the navy would be too ashamed to openly admit what you were able to do, so no one is going to prosecute you for this. And if they did, why, to every army fan in the country, you guys would be heroes, so the navy's not going to publicize that."

I was truly shaken.

"Sergeant Major, we may have trespassed, but the only thing we broke was that padlock, and we would pay for that."

"Mister Carhart, you are getting alarmed about what the Supe might or might not do. But think about that for a minute. Realistically, what could he do, with all the publicity that will be involved, to a Cadet who got caught with the freshly stolen Navy goat at West Point? I don't think he would even *try* to kick you out, and I expect he will calm down in a day or two. Right now, he doesn't know who you are, and if you play this right, he never will. But even if he does find out your names, the only thing you would have to worry about is walking the Area."

"Hunh. Yeah, I guess he would have us walking the Area until graduation."

"Oh, I don't think so. If the Corps ever finds out who you are, why, you guys will be their heroes! And the same goes for every West Point graduate on post: you men did something that they never had the guts to try themselves, and you will be their heroes as well!"

"Well, I don't know. What should we do now?"

"Listen, Mister Carhart, I can't advise you on how to get away with anything, but they may start the confrontations tonight after supper."

'Are they going to confront everyone tonight?"

"No, actually, that's not practical. Colonel Hamblen, the Second Regiment commander, is in Washington right now on another matter, and General Scott has spoken to him on the phone. For some reason, and I don't know what it is, they suspect this was done by a group of Cadets in the First Regiment."

"It wasn't."

"I know, I know. But they say they have evidence and the Com has decided to send officers to confront some first classmen over there in their rooms tonight. And I may as well tell you, one lieutenant colonel who works for the Com is almost bragging that he has figured out who the goat thieves are, they're in the First Regiment and he will have their scalps tonight."

"He's wrong."

"Good, good. But if they come up dry tonight, as you say they will, then they will start on the whole Corps of Cadets tomorrow night. They're going to the rooms of every Cadet who was off post over the weekend and challenge them, ask them, yes or no, whether they know anything about the goat."

"They can't do that, that's using Cadet honor against them, and early in Plebe year we were told that the Tactical Department would never do that."

"I know, I know, and that would also be a violation of Article 15 of the Uniform Code of Military Justice, which applies to every soldier in uniform throughout the army. But the Com is under enormous pressure from the Supe, and he's going to do it. If they come up dry tonight, then tomorrow night, the Com is going to have every tactical officer confront the men in their companies. And as I'm sure you suspect, virtually all the Tacs are on your side, they think this is the best thing that's happened to the Corps of Cadets that any of them can remember. But tomorrow night, that will be their duty, to confront all of you, so be aware of that."

"Sergeant Major, I . . . I don't know what to say . . ."

"Don't say anything, Mister Carhart, this was just a 'heads-up' warning for your group, and I've given you all the information I have. But if you were planning to bring the goat back to West Point anytime soon, I think you might want to accelerate your schedule a little bit."

"Yeah, thank you, Sergeant Major. We'll meet on that tonight."

I no sooner hung up the phone than Art Mosley walked in. "Hey, Tom, what's up?"

He slumped into his chair as I told him what I had just heard.

"Holy cow! Let me call the other guys, we'll have to meet and talk about what we should do real quick!"

After dinner and before our 1:00 p.m. classes, all six of us met in Deme Clainos's room over in North Area. We were all a bit flustered, but soon decided that Bob Lowry would have to call A&C Chevrolet and see if he could get that hemi-engine car we had used in the initial goat theft. If he could, we agreed that several of us would sneak out after Taps, drive up to Eagle Mills and get the goat, then bring him back to West Point. But after that, we had not yet worked out a plan, though we wanted to find a way to present the Navy goat to the football team, probably inside the mess hall. But as we sat in Deme's room talking about it, Art came up with another idea.

"Okay, how about this—we get the goat from the farm and bring him back to West Point. Then we take him out in the woods somewhere near Camp Buckner, tie him to a tree, and dig a big hole."

"What?"

"No, no! Let me finish! We dig a big hole, and there's lots of dead wood on the ground, so we use that to start a big fire in the hole. Once the fire is really going hot, we cut the goat's throat and stick a big spit up his ass, then we cook him, horns and hair and all! After that, we put the cooked goat into a couple of garbage cans, take them to the mess hall, and let the Corps of Cadets eat him!"

Waves of laughter erupted, in which Art joined. But he kept at it.

"Why not? We might as well mark this moment in West Point history with something special that will be remembered! So we steal the Navy goat, then we kill him and we eat him!"

That kept us in stitches for a few minutes and relieved some of the tension we all felt. We decided to figure out the details later, but for now we needed that car again. Lowry called A&C Chevrolet while we waited, and sure enough, it was thumbs-up. He would pick up the car before supper and leave it in the parking lot next to the army gym. After Taps at 11:00 p.m., several of us would sneak out of the Area of Barracks and drive up to Eagle Mills to get the goat.

Bob had to go on this operation because he had the car, and I had to go because I was the only one who knew the way. But Art Mosley and Deme Clainos also insisted on coming along for the ride. Before we left his room, Deme called Captain Slinky, the veterinarian who was charged with caring for the army mules.

Deme told him he and some other Cadets had the goat, which didn't really surprise him because of his earlier questions about goats. Then Deme asked him if we could store the goat in the mule barn, which was up near the football stadium, for a few hours when we brought him back to West Point. Slinky said we could, that he would even hide him in his private bathroom next to his office inside the barn. But he told us to be careful not to tell anyone else, and that he would try to be there to meet us at the barn at 6:00 a.m. Thursday morning.

After Taps at 11:00 p.m., Art and Bob and I put on civilian clothes, then made our way around the back of the mess hall and through the tunnel that got us to North Area with minimal exposure. There we met Deme Clainos and, around 11:30 p.m., headed for the army gym, where Bob had left his car. The most direct route there meant we would have to walk through a brightly lit sallyport that, as always, looked like something out of the Middle Ages.

We were halfway through that sallyport when a loud voice rang out:

"YOU MEN! HALT!"

Uh-oh. We reflexively stopped, pulled our heels together, and stood at attention. A uniformed officer came up beside us, then walked to our front. It was Colonel Hamblen, the Second Regiment commander who, the sergeant major had earlier told me, was at the Pentagon in Washington DC. He was still in uniform at this late hour, and he had probably just gotten back from there and had been inside his office high above one corner of North Area. He looked all four of us dead in the eye like we were criminals.

"It's after Taps. Where do you men think you're going?"

In such a circumstance, the highest-ranking Cadet answers for the group. Bob Lowry, a Cadet captain and regimental adjutant, was the highest-ranking Cadet among us, and he never even hesitated.

"Sir, we are going to a farm in upstate New York to pick up the Navy goat where we left him and bring him back to West Point."

Neither Colonel Hamblen nor any of us even moved for a few seconds. Then he regained his composure.

"All right, men. As you were."

Then Hamblen turned away crisply and walked back into North Area. Elated beyond reason, we virtually flew to the gym parking lot, downright giddy in the realization of what we had just done. We had cowed an army colonel, a West Point regimental commander, and no doubt a future general. Wow! We were so high we felt like we could have flown north on our own, no wings, no engine, no nothing but thrill power! Wow!

The car was the same one we had used only a few days ago, but someone had scrubbed it clean and even sprayed it with some "new car" smell. It was 2:30 a.m. when we reached Eagle Mills, and after ringing the doorbell a few times, my sleepy Uncle Jay appeared. He wiped his eyes as he took us up to the barn, where we found the goat asleep on deep straw in a box stall.

It took us a few minutes to get him up and down to our car. But once we opened the door to the back seat, he eagerly jumped in and lay down, taking up virtually all the space there was. Art carefully got in on the other side, then adjusted himself so that the goat's head and horns were basically in his lap. He didn't mind nuzzling with the goat, he said, but after our earlier car rides with him, he didn't want to be sitting on the other end.

So with Art in the back seat with the goat, Bob driving, and Deme and me sitting on the front bench seat beside him, we headed south.

We didn't get to West Point until just after six o'clock. Cadet reveille was at 5:50 a.m., and by the time we got on post, Cadets were getting ready to march into the mess hall for breakfast.

We drove straight up the hill to the mule barn, and when we got there it was still pitch black, so we got the goat out of the car and led him over to the main barn door. There was a bell, and we rang it, hoping to see Captain Slinky. Instead, a man in a T-shirt pulled the door open for us. We were dumbfounded.

"Is . . . is Captain Slinky here?"

"No, he's not. I'm Sergeant Smith, one of the grooms, and he told me all about this last night, so let me have the goat."

He extended his hand for the ropes, but we hesitated.

"Come on, hurry, up! This door is alarmed and I'm going to have to explain opening it to the M Ps, who will be here soon. Just give me the goat and I'll put him inside Captain Slinky's private bathroom, just like he told me to do."

That was enough for us: the goat went in and Sergeant Smith slid the door back closed. Then Bob drove us down to the army gym parking lot, where we left the car. He put the keys under the driver's floor mat so the A&C Chevrolet people could just pick it up later that afternoon without even seeing any of us. Then we all ran to our rooms and changed for class. We had missed reveille and breakfast formations, but our two Cadet company commanders, Clainos and Mosley, would be able to handle that later. Right now, we were on the edge of a Cadet volcano, and we wanted to make sure it erupted just right.

26

Betrayal

After our first class I walked back to barracks with Art Mosley around 9:00. We had decided to go back to the mule barn around 11:30 a.m. and load the goat back into Bob's car, then take him back to North Area and try to make it in the northside door of the mess hall and figure out some way to get him to the football team. We would probably grab a couple of Plebes who didn't know us, give them the ropes and tell them to run into the section of the mess hall where the football team ate their meals, and let bedlam ensue. This would require several of us to skip yet another class, but by this point we were in so deep that it really didn't matter.

Then as we walked past the commandant's office, I glanced at Sergeant Major Hall's window and saw the "Beat Navy" sticker again.

"Holy shit, Mose! The sticker is in the sergeant major's window! Something's up!"

"Come on, let's go! You can call him from my room."

We didn't run, but we walked fast. I dialed his number and he picked it up after one ring.

"Sergeant Major, this is Mister Carhart. What has happened?"

"Mister Carhart, they've got the goat! The military police are up at the mule barn right now, and they're getting ready to drive him back to Annapolis."

"What?"

"I'm sorry, but someone turned you in. Somehow the Com found out an hour ago that the goat had been put in the mule barn earlier this morning. So now, like I said, there's a bunch of military policemen up there guarding everything, and they're forming a caravan for the trip. It's going to be commanded by a full colonel, so they are going all out."

"Okay. Thanks."

I let my limp hand fall in my lap, but Art was still in the dark.

"What happened?"

"They got the goat."

"What?"

"That's what I said. They got the goat. The sergeant major told me somebody stabbed us in the back and the Com found out he is at the mule barn about an hour ago. Now he says the place is crawling with MPs and they're forming a caravan to drive him back to Annapolis."

"A caravan?"

"That's what he said, a caravan, I guess of army trucks. And a full colonel is going to be in command."

"Holy shit!"

"Yeah, I know."

I stood up.

"But they haven't left yet. Come on, let's take Lowry's car and go up there."

We raced up the hill past Lusk Reservoir, drove past the big white mule barn, then parked fifty yards downhill. And sure enough, when we walked up to it, trying to look as casual as we could, there seemed to be a cloud of MPs everywhere. We both walked up to the main door as if we belonged there but were blocked by three or four burly soldiers with MP shoulder bands, one of whose arms were also covered with stripes. He spoke up.

"Sorry, mister, you can't go in there."

"But sergeant, I just want to . . ."

"No, sorry, no Cadets are allowed in there now. Are you men mule riders?"

Certain Cadets who were already good horseback riders when they got to West Point had volunteered to ride the mules during football games and other ceremonies. After their horsemanship was tested, each year several Cadets from each class became official mule riders and rode the four army mules into the stadium at football games. And if they wanted to, the mule riders also had special access to the mule barn during the week in order to care for their mounts, or at least pretend to—that, after all, was the job of the veterinarian and his soldier staff. Mose didn't answer the sergeant's question but instead stalled.

"Listen, sergeant, I don't think you understand, we just want to . . ."

But the sergeant wasn't even listening as he held out his arms to bar our entrance.

"Different rules now, mister. We have been told to keep all Cadets away from the mule barn, even mule riders, so I'm afraid you men will just have to go back down to the Area of Barracks, maybe come back later today or tomorrow. We've got a big operation underway, and you must keep away."

We turned and started to walk back down the hill. But as we did, we walked along the side of the mule barn, only we were gradually walking down below the first floor. There was a door out of this lower level, covered by an asphalt-covered roof that stuck out maybe ten feet from the building and was supported by two white posts at our end. Above it was a window.

Art and I looked at each other and knew we weren't about to pass that up—maybe we could get in through the window, and after that would see what we could do about getting the goat, if we found him, back out through the same window. We both shinnied up one of the posts and climbed on top of the small roof. And when we looked in the window, the Navy goat looked back. Holy cow! He was inside a small room with a toilet behind him, and the door was closed. This must be Slinky's private bathroom. We tried to raise the window with our hands, but it was locked. What should we do?

"Mose, I'll jump down and find a rock, then you break the window and raise it. I'll climb back up here and . . ."

A loud shout from up the hill snapped our heads around. "Hey!"

It was the MP sergeant who had looked around the corner and seen us. Then he and the other MPs falling in behind him were headed our way. We both jumped down, then ran for the car. The MPs, not quite sure who we were, seemed to give up once we moved away from the mule barn. As we drove back down the hill, we tried to figure out what to do next. Mose was adamant:

"I didn't come this far and run all those risks just to see the whole thing disappear like so much smoke!"

I felt the same way.

"I'm with you, Mose. But now they've got the damned goat and we can't get it back."

"Yeah, I know. And if we had brought that goat into the mess hall, the Corps would have gone crazy!"

"So it looks like we have lost the whole shebang, especially the morale boost we all would have gotten, and that's just not right."

"Let's get our group together before lunch, and try to figure out something we can do. I'll call around when we get back to my room, but for now we'll just leave the car in the gym parking lot again."

It was still mid-period when we got to Art's room, and within minutes the other four guys were there, all of us somewhat crestfallen. Lowry was the last to arrive, and when he closed the door it was as if we were all smothering in a gray cloud of gloom. Art spoke first:

"All right, who told anyone outside our group?"

We all protested our innocence, and then Mike Brennan took over.

"Listen, guys, we don't need this, and I'm sure none of us talked. It was probably some Cadet who listened at a closed door and wanted to kiss up to his Tac, so he turned us in."

Mosley wouldn't stop.

"I'll tell you who snitched on us, some back-stabbing coward, that's who!"

And Clainos wouldn't leave it alone.

"Yeah, some ass-kissing opportunist! And we all know there *are* Cadets like that!"

True enough, we all did. Still, the Supe didn't yet know who we were, and he was probably deliriously happy just because he had gotten the goat back alive and could ship it home to Annapolis. That probably meant that if we did nothing at all, the whole thing would just be forgotten by the authorities at West Point.

But none of us were happy with that. If we made a scene of some sort, of course, that might give us away, and there could be hell to pay. And we had all heard what the sergeant major had told me, that the Supe told the Com that if he found out who we were he would have us prosecuted for trespass, and if we weren't convicted that he would have us dismissed from the academy. Deme Clainos, however, just didn't buy it.

"He's not going to have us prosecuted, that would be too big an embarrassment for the navy—it would be the army dueling the navy in federal court, all because some stupid Cadets, not even officers yet, were able to defeat their supposedly sophisticated security measures! That's the sort of big public black eye that the navy just doesn't want, so they won't do that!"

Mosley chimed in.

"And the Supe is not going to kick us out either, there would be a public uproar if he even tried! I'm telling you, this whole goat theft deal will give West Point a better public image than anything that's happened up here since World War II!"

None of us really bought into that, and our groans said so.

"Oh, come on Mosley!"

"You're reaching there, Art!"

Maybe he was, but the act itself was really quite bold, and it had been a long time since West Point Cadets had shown their spunk so publicly. But we were still confused, and I said so.

"So what do we do?"

Brennan spoke up.

"I don't know, but I think we need to somehow fall on our swords in public, let the Corps know that we had stolen the goat and brought him all the way back here, only to get caught at the very last minute. But whatever we do, we need to do it fast, right now. Before all the energy we feel disappears, we need to get that same energy into all other Cadets."

I couldn't quite understand what he was saying.

"Look, we've got class in twenty minutes, and it's now less than two hours before dinner formation. So you're saying we should do something inside the mess hall? I don't see how we could, everything in there is so structured."

As a regimental adjutant, Lowry was with me.

"I'm afraid that's right, no one of us could just walk up to the poop deck and grab the microphone. Hell, we couldn't even get up those stairs unless it was scheduled."

Mosley agreed.

"Yeah, that's right. And even if one of us could get up there and grab the mike, the officer in charge who eats there would just pull the mike's cord out of the socket, and after it went dead he would just take it away. And fry whoever had made the attempt."

But Mewhinney had an idea.

"Listen, we're all in agreement that we don't care if our names come out and we get in big trouble, lose our privileges for the rest of Firsty year, and end up walking the Area for a long time, right?"

We all nodded and mumbled our assent.

"Okay, then how about this: we get one of those portable loudspeakers the cheerleaders use and right before dinner formation, all six of us get on top of that Dempsey Dumpster right by South Area. It is right below the Com's office, and more than half the Corps comes back from class that way, everyone who lives in Old South, New South, or Central Area, right?"

We nodded in agreement, not sure where this was headed.

Betrayal

"Okay. Now, at about 11:40, the first Cadets will start coming back from class and walking right past the Dumpster. So we enlist some Yearlings to start yelling that there's a surprise rally in Old South at 11:55, ten minutes before dinner formation. It's the biggest football weekend coming up, so that would not be unusual. We can certainly get all the Plebes there before they even know that it's for anything more than a big rally. And there's still a big mystery among Cadets about the Navy goat. So we tell the Yearlings to say there will be news about the goat. Then when we've got a big enough crowd, we pick up the loudspeaker and confess."

Lowry was astounded.

"You mean we just tell them we stole the Navy goat, right there in front of the whole corps, with the Com looking down on us?"

"Yes, I do! Why not? You got any other plan?"

It was a bitter pill to swallow, but we were all in this together, as Brennan reminded us.

"Remember, guys, before we left the Actons to try to get the goat, we all put our hands in a circle and agreed that this would be all for one and one for all! That means if one of us gets caught, we all get caught!"

The air was suddenly thinner, and the glumness seemed almost to evaporate. Mosley spoke up.

"Okay, then, I guess that's what we'll do. I can get a megaphone, that's easy."

Clainos was watching the time.

"Okay, let's get a move on, class in ten minutes."

Mosley sneered.

"Wait a minute, with all we've got on the line, I'm not going to class! First thing I'm going to do is get that loudspeaker. Tom, are you with me?"

Skipping class at West Point was major risk, for if you got caught—and attendance was taken and turned in at the beginning of every class—the result would be a commandant's board, and the punishment accorded for such an outrageous act—skipping class—was twenty-two demerits, forty-four punishment tours, and two months' special confinement. That meant that, in addition to spending your Wednesday and Saturday afternoons walking the Area, you really never got out of your room after class, which was indescribably tedious and painful, especially on weekends.

"Yeah, Mose, I'm with you! Let's go!"

27

Falling on Our Swords

By 11:40 a.m. we had arranged for a half-dozen Yearlings to act as criers, alerting all Cadets coming back from class that there would be a rally in South Area before dinner formation and that the Navy goat was involved. We even sent some of them over in front of the mess hall to catch Cadets who lived in North Area. Within ten minutes or so, there were probably five hundred Cadets in Old South Area, wondering aloud if they would see the Navy goat. The six of us were assembled atop the Dempsey Dumpster. As the lowest-ranking Cadet with the least to lose—what, are they going to take my one stripe away?—I stepped forward, picked up the handset, and turned it on.

"Beat Navy!"

I was amazed at how loudly my voice echoed from the granite walls all around us, but the response of the crowd of Cadets was deafening.

"Beat Navy!"

I looked off to my left fifty feet at the back side of the commandant's office, which rose four floors like the barracks of which it formed the end. There were four floors of windows, and all were filled with faces staring intently down on me. I turned back to the crowd.

"We called this rally today because we want you to know that the six of us—"

I turned and waved my arm to include the other five men.

"—went down to Annapolis last weekend, or I should say to the Severna Park Naval Security Station. Without boring you with the details, suffice it to say that we distracted the Marine guards with pretty girls, then broke into his pen and stole the Navy goat!"

The volcano erupted and Cadets were suddenly jumping all over themselves.

"We want the goat! We want the goat!"

I raised my arm and stilled the crowd.

"Last night we went to the nearby farm where we had stored him and brought him to West Point just after reveille, then stashed him in the mule barn."

A crowd of a dozen or so Plebes started running toward the steps that led up the hill toward the chapel, a half mile beyond which was the mule barn, and I turned the mike toward them.

"No, no! Wait! It's too late!"

The surprised Plebes turned and looked at me, stunned by my words.

"While we were in class this morning someone ratted on us, and when we went up to get him and bring him down to the mess hall an hour ago, there were MPs everywhere and we couldn't get near the place. Since then, a caravan of army trucks left post to take the goat back to Annapolis, so it's too late for us to get him back. But we just wanted you to know that we really did steal the Navy goat, we had him right here and came within a hair of giving him to the Corps in anticipation of beating Navy on Saturday!"

Loud cheers boomed out from the crowd. But by this time a colonel in formal class "A" uniform had come around the corner from the Com's office and was headed our way, As he got closer, the cheers were replaced with booing by Cadets: here comes The Man! But he ignored the crowd noise and confronted each of us as we got down. None of us tried to get away, for we had already agreed that we would all take the hit, whatever it was, together. I came down first and he tried to stare me down, but I smiled at him and his voice actually trembled as he spoke.

Falling on Our Swords

"I don't know what you men think you're doing, but I'll have your names and companies."

I was enormously composed and relaxed after my brief words to the crowd of Cadets.

"Sure, sir. Carhart, T.M., Company E-2."

He had a small pad of paper, and as he tried to write, his fingers trembled, so I repeated my name more slowly.

"That's Carhart, C . . . a . . . r . . ."

I paused for a few seconds, as his entire hands were now shaking so hard that he couldn't even write. He stopped, flexed his fingers, and cleared his throat.

"You say C . . . a . . . r . . ."

I waited until he had those three letters written.

"Yes, sir, C . . . a . . . r . . . h . . . a . . . r . . . t. Initials T.M., Company E-2."

"Okay. Next?

"Mosley, A.C., that's M . . . o . . . s . . . l . . . e . . . y. Initials A.C., also Company E-2."

By now the colonel seemed to have recovered and was easily writing our names, and obviously they were for the Com. And then, of course, for the Supe. Well, they had the damned goat back because someone had stabbed us in the back, so let them do what they would. At that moment, we were impervious to punishment, whatever it might be. And we knew it, for we had carried off a daring plot as Cadets that none of these older officers, during their own Cadet days, had ever even attempted, nor, indeed, ever would have attempted. For that alone, we could look down on them all. And while so doing, we could smile.

After he took the last man's name, the colonel told us that we would hear from the commandant's office "in due course." Then we were released, and as we walked back to our company formations for dinner, other Cadets were bouncing all around us, cheering and clapping us on the back. This was not unexpected, but I had never before felt such a sense of pure elation. And clearly, as our names were taken, all six of us had felt some invisible mantle of power and authority descend on our shoulders. In the West Point world, as was obvious to all, we had just figuratively run the ball a hundred yards for the winning touchdown.

And it felt great!

The Army-Navy game was a hoot, and after the Cadets and middies had entered the stands on opposite sides of the field, there was a pause in the festivities while we waited for the football teams to come out on the field. At that moment, a black limousine rolled onto the field and stopped in front of the Army side. Out of it jumped a half-dozen men in black wearing black sunglasses, obviously middies in costume, who looked around, as if to make sure the stage was clear. They waved and signaled each other, then two of them went back to the limo and opened the door again, reached in, and out came Billy XIV, his bright white coat gleaming and his blue and gold horns shining in the sun. They guided him with ropes around his neck and trotted back across the field to the Navy side. As they did so, the front row of middies unrolled a long white paper sign. Perhaps fifty or sixty feet long and three or four feet high, it said in bold letters:

For it is written:

This sign was passed upward in the stands to the rows of middies above and behind them, making for a slowly ascendant warning. After it had gone ten or twelve rows and continued its journey, another sign was unrolled by the front row of middies and followed the first one upward in the stands. This one read:

Thou shalt not steal

We all got a good laugh out of that, but unfortunately, the game ended in a dismal 7–7 tie, which has appropriately been analogized to kissing your sister. Still, it was a Saturday night away from West Point, and that night in Philadelphia, we all ate and drank our fill.

Particularly the latter.

Falling on Our Swords

28

The Shadow of the Guillotine

When we returned to West Point on Sunday after the game, Christmas vacation was not far away. And while we had academic concerns about tests after the holiday, we were also worried about our looming punishment for having stolen the Navy goat. And sure enough, on December 1, 1965, the Wednesday after our return, all six of us were ordered to report to the commandant's office at 4:00 p.m. and appear before a commandant's board, the highest level of disciplinary review at the academy.

Although known as a commandant's board, such boards did not actually involve the commandant himself. Rather, it normally consisted of one colonel and two lieutenant colonels, and these officers decided cases involving serious violations of Cadet regulations, including administration of specific punishment for guilty Cadets. None of us had ever heard of a Com's board that resulted in dismissal of charges, for most Cadets who appeared before them had been caught red-handed. Instead, the punishments they assessed would be quite severe, with a minimum of twenty-two demerits, forty-four punishment tours, and two months' special confinement (except for class, meals, and formations, a Cadet must stay inside his room). If serious enough, punishment for the offense could even reach actual expulsion from the academy. In other words, although we believed our special circumstances warranted lesser treatment, the calling of a commandant's board meant that we were in very hot water.

Upon arrival, we were directed to the second floor. There, a major told us that we were to enter a conference room one by one and report to a special board of four colonels. That was a little bit unsettling, as none of us had ever heard of a commandant's board that included more than one colonel.

The commandant's office was inside a nineteenth-century building attached to the southeastern corner of Central Area. This meant it was right at a choke point for Cadet traffic to and from the academic buildings, and we all walked by it several times each day. It was on the second floor and consisted not only of the Com's personal office, but also of an array of other smaller offices inhabited by staff officers, a small conference room, and a host of female secretaries.

Unlike the Cadet world in the middle of which it was sited, this was a quiet space with hard-wood wall paneling, heavy drapes, and thick carpeting. These solemn and sober features only added to the distress felt by Cadets in that location while awaiting commandant's boards.

Like us.

West Point has long been renowned for strict regulations, rigid discipline, and severe punishment. All Cadets were inspected in their rooms and in ranks several times each week, and these were always serious and risky moments. For normal transgressions like poorly shined shoes or dust in rifle barrel, demerits were issued by the company tactical officer, and too many demerits meant hours walking the Area with rifle on shoulder during normally free time.

But if a Cadet was caught performing any of an array of more serious offenses, such as skipping a class, missing a Sunday chapel formation, or possessing illegal liquor in his room, then he would have to appear before a commandant's board. He would there be confronted with his acts and, if found guilty (almost always the case since the perpetrator usually would have been caught in the act), he would be subjected to more serious punishment.

Com's boards only met every few weeks or months, and their decisions would be announced in the mess hall as a sort of warning to all other Cadets. Usually, these announcements were not of great interest and passed with little comment. But some exploits, such as getting caught after Taps both off post and dead drunk brought waves of hooting and laughter from Cadets. And one such announcement early in our Yearling year had practically brought down the house.

As part of prescribed "Army Orientation Training," all Cadets were assigned to different U.S. Army units in Germany for four weeks during one summer. They would there fill the duties of an army lieutenant and platoon leader, this to give them a taste of what lay in store for them after graduation. While this was generally considered a valuable experience that we all looked forward to, there were moments when Cadets performing that duty showed that they lacked certain social graces. And so it was that, during the early fall of our Yearling year, we heard the following announcement in the mess hall about a Firsty we will call Cadet John Doe:

Attention to Orders: During the month of July 1963, as part of the Army Orientation Training program, Cadet John Doe was assigned to an element of the First Armored Division in a U.S. Army Caserne outside of Munich, Germany. On 22 July 1963, Cadet Doe did enter the city of Munich in the company of lieutenants from the First Armored Division. Cadet X did then and thereupon consume numerous alcoholic beverages. At about 2300 hours, while knowing that an adjoining building was a house of ill repute, Cadet X did intentionally throw a U.S. Army M-46 smoke grenade through an open window of said building. Said M-46 smoke grenade did not only produce great volumes of smoke inside said building, but it also ignited a fire which resulted in the rapid exit of a considerable number of German men and women into the midtown street from said building while wearing less than proper attire, and the subsequent arrival of German fire trucks. Cadet Doe was arrested by German police and charged with destruction of furniture and other property, including damage to the structure of said building, caused by the fire he ignited by intentionally throwing said smoke grenade into said building. Under the provisions of the Status of Forces Treaty between the United States of America and the Federal Republic of Germany, Cadet Doe was transferred to the custody of U.S. Army military police from the First Armored Division and from there to the U.S. Military Academy. By his actions, Cadet Doe has brought considerable discredit and disgrace upon the image of the United States Military Academy, the United States Army, and the United States of America. On 5 September 1963, a commandant's board reviewed this matter and found Cadet Doe guilty of the alleged offenses, for which he is now awarded 88 demerits, 176 punishment tours, and one year of special confinement.

The Corps of Cadets just erupted in delight, and although he had a long and difficult punishment before him, for that night Cadet John Doe was our hero. His was the biggest "slug" we had heard of, and his exploits promptly became part of Cadet legend.

But Cadet Doe had not been dismissed, and so memory of his story was somewhat reassuring as we awaited our turns to be strapped to the guillotine. If the extreme acts of Cadet Doe had not resulted in his dismissal, we thought, how could they justify dismissing us for only stealing the Navy goat?

We just didn't know, so it was a silent and glum wait.

Then the major opened the door for us and we went in and reported in order of Cadet rank. Bob Lowry went first, his three Cadet captain's stripes on his arms with the adjutant's three matching rocker stripes below them showing his high rank. Then the three Cadet captain company commanders wearing three stripes on their arms, Art Mosley, Mike Brennan, and Deme Clainos, went through the same door one by one. After

them, Mike Mewhinney, wearing the two stripes of a Cadet lieutenant, went in and reported. And last of all, it was my turn, my
single stripe marking me as a lowly Cadet sergeant.

After reporting, we were directed to a row of chairs, and as
the last man in I sat at the end. We were inside a conference
room and the colonels were seated behind a long table facing
us, each with a pen and paper in front of him. Then one of the
colonels, Jack Morris, commanding officer of the First Regiment, USCC, opened the proceedings.

"Gentlemen, the six of you are accused of committing two
offenses on November 20, 1965: first is a violation of specific
Cadet limits by entering the Annapolis, Maryland, area, and second, a criminal trespass onto the grounds of a highly restricted
U.S. Navy research and communications facility known as the
Severna Park Naval Security Station. For that second offense,
you would normally face a general court-martial. However, the
commandant of Cadets, General Scott, has arranged for your
court-martial to take an unusual form, and that is why you are
appearing today before this board of four colonels. Should we
find you guilty of these offenses, we will make recommendations to the commandant as to your punishment. Do you all
understand those charges?"

We did.

"The first alleged offense is the violation of specific regulations in that you went to an area near the U.S. Naval Academy
in Annapolis, Maryland, an area that, during the time in question, had been specifically made 'Off Limits' to all West Point
Cadets, with the threat of severe punishment for any violations.
The superintendent made sure all Cadets were made aware of
this restriction on their travel liberties on or about November
21, 1965. Do you all remember that restriction?"

We did.

"And do you all understand that charge of violation of Regulations, USCC?"

We did.

"All right. Now, in addition to the charge of violation of Cadet regulations, you are also charged with a federal offense, which is criminal trespass onto the grounds of a very high security U.S. Navy installation and the removal of U.S. Navy property therefrom. That property would be the Navy goat. Now this added charge is of a violation of federal law, for which the punishment can include lengthy incarceration. The area onto which you trespassed was supposedly sealed off from the public by two large concentric fences that are supposedly very openly marked with 'No Trespassing' signs. Passage beyond these fences could only have been legitimately made by individuals showing the appropriate U.S. Navy passes while going through gates manned twenty-four hours each day by United States Marine guards. You are accused of somehow avoiding these gates and making your way inside both fences without proper authorization, thus making your presence there one of criminal trespass. Do you all understand this second charge?"

We did

"Okay, good. Now, quite frankly, men, we have never conducted this sort of investigation before, and it is rather unusual. As you know, under Article 15 of the Uniform Code of Military Justice, we cannot force you to testify against yourselves. So what we have decided, along with the commandant, is that we will give you a choice: you can either agree to tell us everything, all the details of what happened when you stole the goat; or you can choose to remain silent. We will judge your culpability whether you agree to tell us what happened or not, but you should understand that our punishment recommendations to the commandant will be less severe if you are candid with us. We would prefer that you tell us everything, but we'll leave that up to you. Do you men all understand that?"

We did.

"Okay, we're going to give you some time right now to talk among yourselves and decide whether or not to tell us what happened. Unfortunately, we are really unprepared for this sort of operation because, as I said, it has never happened before. So what I propose is that the four of us, the board of colonels, will go down the hall and have a cup of coffee while you men discuss this among yourselves. Does that sound satisfactory to you?"

It did.

"Good. Okay, you men are free to discuss this for as long as you need. We hope you will choose to share the details with us, as that will make our job much easier, but again, we leave that decision entirely up to you. When you have made your decision, Major Hankins will be in the hall waiting for you, so you tell him and he will get us and we will rejoin you."

Colonel Morris turned, eyebrows raised, to face a major seated near the door.

"Jerry, you heard that, didn't you?"

Major Hankins stood and nodded as he answered.

"Yes, sir, I did."

"Okay, then, we will adjourn for the time being. Jerry, sit outside the door and wait."

The four colonels left, and once alone, our decision was quick. Deme Clainos spoke first.

"Anybody want to hold out?"

Mosley jumped in.

"What interest would that serve? After our little Dempsey Dumpster show, we have already admitted that we did it, so what benefit could come from holding out?"

None of us could see any, and Brennan spoke next.

"All right, so who is going to speak to the colonels for us?"

All eyes turned to me, but I didn't want that, so I answered.

"I'm not the leader, Mike, you are. You heard what Mr. Acton said, you are Jason and Helen is Medea."

But Mosley wouldn't let me go.

"Carhart, this was your idea in the first place, you've been in on everything."

Then Mewhinney chimed in.

"And Carhart, when you got there Saturday night, we were all ready to quit, and I thought you were drunk."

I shrugged and smiled.

"I probably was, but just a little bit."

"Well, whether you were drunk or not, you insisted on making a recon run, so Lowry and Clainos and Mosley went with you, and you found that open gate. If you hadn't done that, we would have come back empty-handed!"

And Art Mosley put the cap on it.

"Carhart, we're all Cadet captains and you're the only Cadet sergeant. They had us report in by rank, so you came last, and it would just blow their minds if they come back and see that the lowest-ranking guy in the group is our spokesman!"

I tried to protest but the rest of them hooted me down, so I agreed to speak for the group. On the wall to our left was a blackboard, and before we called the colonels back, I made a drawing of the security station as best I remembered it. Then we sent(!) Major Hankins down the hall to get the colonels.

When they came back in and sat down, we had rearranged our seats so that, rather than being on the end, I was sitting in the middle. Then I stood up.

"Sirs, we have decided to tell you everything, and I have been chosen to speak for all us."

The colonels looked at each other, but Colonel Morris nodded approvingly.

"Good, good. I will assure you that with your candor we will look more favorably upon your alleged offenses. Proceed."

I started earlier that fall, when Deme Clainos and I had been hospital patients in adjoining beds and the idea of stealing the Navy goat was first aired, and Colonel Morris interrupted me.

"So, if you men had been treated in separate rooms, none of this would have ever occurred, correct?"

"Sir ... I guess I just can't answer that ..."

"That's all right, Mister Carhart, I was just noting that in passing. Proceed."

As I went through our early organization days, I said that two of the original volunteers had decided at the last minute, after we had made our recon run, to drop out, though I did not say their names. But after all, since they had not gone through the fence with us, they had neither broken any Cadet regulations nor committed criminal trespass on a federal whatever-it-was, so they were clean and were not mentioned again.

When I got to the part where we broke the padlock and went into the goat pen while the girls flirted with the Marine guards, two of the colonels covered their faces with their hands, obviously smothering laughter. And again, when the girls' car broke down and Mose and I hitchhiked to West Point early Sunday morning, there was more suppressed laughter. The longer I spoke, the better I felt, and when I finished, all four colonels were smiling or openly hiding their laughter. Then I finished by asking if any of them had any questions.

At first, the four colonels looked at each other blankly.

Then Colonel Maertens, who commanded the Third Regiment, USCC, spoke up.

"Mister Carhart, if the Navy goat had not been found in the mule barn, we heard that you had plans to kill the goat, then cook him and somehow try to feed him to the Corps of Cadets in the mess hall. Is there any truth to that?"

I gulped hard, but then Art Mosley spoke up.

"I suggested that, sir, but it was only a joke. Probably some Cadet in the hallway was listening at the door when I said it and reported it to a tactical officer, but it was just a joke."

So maybe that's how word got to the Com that the goat was in the mule barn—some Cadet overheard us talking about it and wanted to get ahead with the Tacs, so he turned us in.

Next was Colonel Gobstok, who worked for the Supe.

"Mister Carhart, I have served a long career in the Corps of Engineers, and I have a purely professional question. The bolt cutters that you say you borrowed from the post engineers and then you say you think you dropped them in the grass and couldn't remember where they were—that's a pretty valuable piece of equipment, so did you ever find it?"

Bolt cutters? What kind of a question was that? Is that all you can think of? They might be worth maybe a few hundred bucks, and because they were used in the successful theft of the Navy goat, who cares? But fortunately I had an answer.

"Yes, sir, when we were taking the goat through the pedestrian gate, Mister Mewhinney was last. As I told you, he was the one who thought to loop the broken padlock through the hasp of the goat pen, and he did the same with the padlock on that pedestrian gate. And I forgot to say that while he was doing that, he also saw the bolt cutters I had dropped in the grass, so he picked them up and put them in the trunk of the car before we left."

Colonel Morris, who would later become a three-star lieutenant general and the chief of engineers, had one last question.

"Mister Carhart, we've all seen the Navy goat at 'The Game,' and that's a big animal with long horns. How did you ever get him inside a sedan car with all six of you?"

"Sir, I don't know, but all I can say is just that, somehow, we did. And I will tell you that during our escape, he shit and peed all over us, so it was not a fun ride."

This time the colonels all had to smother their laughter with their hands. Then Colonel Morris stood up and the rest of us followed his lead.

"All right, gentlemen, this concludes your part of our Special Commandant's Board and Amended Court-Martial proceeding. We will review the information you have given us, decide on an appropriate punishment for you, and submit our report to the commandant. You will all hear from the commandant in due course."

29

The Commandant of Cadets

We were somewhat upbeat when we left, none of us more so than Mosley, who predicted no punishment at all. But he was also the guy who had wanted to kill the goat, then cook it and eat it, so you never could tell what Mose was thinking.

Christmas leave was less than three weeks away, and we had an academic load that just would not quit. Because of that, we thought we would not hear from the Com until after we got back from Christmas leave. But then, only two days after our "Amended Court-Martial proceeding," we all received orders to report to the commandant on Thursday, December 9, at 1600 hours.

Our commandant's board presided over by four colonels had taken place in a conference room within the confines of the commandant's office. Over the years, many commandants had come and gone, most of them to rise in rank after their departure, for that was probably the most prestigious post for a brigadier general in the U.S. Army. And now, we would actually enter the Com's private office and see him face-to-face.

While many Cadets had faced commandant's boards for disciplinary issues, these were ordinarily presided over, as mentioned earlier, by a colonel and lieutenant colonels. But we knew that very few Cadets ever went inside the commandant's personal office except on celebratory occasions, so we were in a very special situation. And we were there to receive punishment, not to celebrate, so we gritted our teeth.

That morning at breakfast a certain concern was expressed by members of all classes, for the *New York Times* had published a Defense Intelligence Agency—a sort of mini-CIA inside the Pentagon—report that had obviously been leaked by an insider. And the report was the result of an intensive study into the effect of Operation Rolling Thunder, which was the ongoing campaign of bombing North Vietnam. According to that report, the bombing had failed in its two main efforts, which were to destabilize the North Vietnamese economy and to appreciably diminish the flow of arms and men into South Vietnam. Any further belief that such bombing might ever have either effect was, in the words of the report, a "colossal misjudgment." And that was the war that awaited us.

At 4:00 p.m. the six of us arrived outside the commandant's office. After reporting in, we were told that we would each be called in to speak to the commandant individually, and that while awaiting our turn we were to be seated in a row of chairs outside his door. This was a formal area with thick carpeting and elaborate wood paneling that, over the years, had seen many commandants come and go, so just by being there we were touching West Point history.

Once again, we sat by Cadet rank. Soon enough, Bob Lowry's name was called, and he went through the door and closed it behind him. We could only faintly hear his voice through the heavy wood:

"Sir, Mister Lowry reports to the commandant of Cadets as ordered."

After that, though our ears were eagerly perked, we heard nothing, for the Com was obviously speaking in a conversational tone inaudible to us. Then within only a few minutes, the door opened and Bob came out. We got a closed-mouth smile from him as he walked by, but nothing more, as we really couldn't talk in this formal, august area. Then it was Mosley's turn.

I agonized as each man went into the Com's office, then came out within only a few minutes and silently disappeared down the hall. Finally, it was my turn, so I walked through the door and closed it, then stood at attention as I saluted.

"Sir, Mister Carhart reports to the commandant of Cadets as ordered."

General Scott sat impassively behind his desk as he returned my salute.

"At ease, Mister Carhart. I won't take up much of your time, and I will say virtually the same thing to you that I have said to your co-conspirators. I have read the detailed report submitted to me by the four colonels who constituted your commandant's board, and I have spoken to all of them in some detail. After a full appraisal, and as one West Pointer to another, I can only say to you, as I have said to your classmates in this operation, those magical words from our alma mater: Well done. I am sure you will do very well in the army, and I would be proud to have you serve under me. It's hard to predict a Cadet's performance after graduation, but you men have given us strong evidence that you have learned a lot here about military operations. You certainly know how to conduct a dangerous raid, and you have shown an extraordinary amount of courage and persistence in the face of the unknown, as well as the ability to think on your feet under pressure."

He paused, and words jumped out of my mouth.

"Thank you, sir."

"You're welcome. But those are just my personal comments. From the reports I have received, you men have violated Cadet regulations as well as federal law, so as commandant of Cadets, I must deliver some punishment. Therefore, I have decided to remove your first class privileges from now until January 8, 1966—one month from today. Do you understand?"

Wow! Removal of my first class privileges? You mean I can't do such things as go to the movies during the week, which I had only rarely done before? And for one lousy month, including the week we would be gone on Christmas leave? Wow! I found myself suddenly and unashamedly smiling.

"Yes, sir, I understand."

"All right. But one more thing, Mister Carhart. The other men involved in this operation are Cadet captains and one lieutenant, while you are only a Cadet sergeant, correct?"

"Yes, sir."

"Well, don't worry about that too much. We have learned that the ways in which Cadets get promoted don't always indicate much about their future in the military or in life. And just because the tactical department doesn't think you are a very good West Point Cadet does not mean you will not flourish both in the army and beyond. Do you understand that?"

"Yes, sir, I do."

"Good. And remember, the two most illustrious West Point graduates ever are General Ulysses Grant, who commanded the Union Army that won the Civil War, and General Dwight Eisenhower, who commanded the U.S. Army that won World War II in Europe. And as of today, those are the only two men who have served consecutive terms as Republican presidents of the United States. Did you know that?"

"No, sir."

"Well, now you do. So if you graduate as a Cadet sergeant, remember that Grant and Eisenhower also both graduated as Cadet sergeants. And so you will be in very good company."

"Thank you again, sir."

"You are welcome, Mister Carhart. But before you go, I must say that this was a splendid feat you men pulled off, and I believe you will all fly high and far. Now get out of here."

I didn't walk out of his office, I soared. The other five guys were waiting outside, and in a very unusual Cadet act in Central Area, we all hugged and hooted our joy. The glow lasted for a long time, but performance of the act itself had given us great strength, so much so that, as we gradually realized, the only rules in life that would ever restrain us would be the ones we made ourselves. And with such a "Mission Impossible" behind us, we absolutely knew that, with proper planning, preparation, and guts, anything we might ever want in life, no matter how intimidating or unobtainable it might seem, could readily be made to fall within our grasps.

Winston Churchill once gave a graduation address at Sandhurst, the British equivalent of West Point. He spoke only three words, and he said them again and again and again: "Never give up. Never give up. Never give up. . . ." This was a message for the ages. It became Churchill's adage that he followed along with his nation as they fought World War II. The British did not give up. After Pearl Harbor, Germany declared war on the United States, and so we entered the lists in Europe, and our weight, along with that of Russia, was enough to turn the tide. And Churchill's advice endured: Never give up.

While we cannot begin to compare our minor exploit to the ferocious violence of war, neither did we give up. This stood us in good stead as we transitioned from cadet to regular army officer. It helped to develop the character that life sometimes demands. It tested us. It brought a challenge that forced us to look deep into our hearts seeking the better decision. The memory is fresh and vivid, and the pure joy to be found in having once been an Argonaut will always remain.

After graduation, all six of us would serve in Vietnam. Thereafter, four of us left the army while two remained in the ranks as their primary career. So let's take a closer look and see if these men gained anything of enduring value from their high-risk adventure as young men.

30

Vietnam Veterans Memorial

Right after graduation Art Mosley went to Harvard, where he earned an MBA, then used his economic skills as a staff planning officer in Vietnam. Upon his return to the U.S., he left the army and got involved in commercial real estate, which included the construction of office buildings and a planned residential community in Maryland. Then in the spring of 1980, he got a call from a West Point classmate, Jack Wheeler, who also had an MBA from Harvard.

The phone call came because Jack had just read an article in the *Washington Post* about a Vietnam veteran named Jan Scruggs, who was trying to build a memorial to Vietnam veterans in Washington DC. Scruggs had founded the Vietnam Veterans Memorial Fund (VVMF), a charitable organization that existed largely on paper, for Scruggs had only been able to raise $144. But this cause was very attractive to Wheeler, and in his call to Mosley he asked him to join in helping Scruggs.

Art dutifully joined VVMF as a volunteer, and right away he saw that it had virtually no structure or organization of any kind. He told Jack and Jan that there could be no more catch-as-catch-can, and if they wanted to succeed, they needed to operate like a business. He thereupon wrote an organizational chart with six subcommittees and a master chronology detailing each step toward raising $10 million and dedicating the memorial in November 1982.

Soon enough, with half a dozen part-time worker bees, these two smart West Point and Harvard graduates had been able to secure from Congress a license to build a memorial on the Mall "in honor and recognition of the men and women of the United States military who served in the Vietnam War." Congress also gave VVMF a plot of land on the Mall near the Lincoln Memorial as a site for their proposed Vietnam veterans memorial.

I was then a bureaucrat inside the Pentagon, and it wasn't long before Mosley called me with the same pitch, knowing I would be eager to help. I went to their offices and was readily recruited. The only thing of any value that I did for them, however, was to get an unsecured loan for $45,000 (a lot of money in the early eighties) from a big DC bank, this to pay for a mass mailing. But after that and a few months stuffing envelopes, I dropped out of the effort.

Then an open competition was announced for the design of the Vietnam Veterans Memorial, with the only requirement being that it had to list the names of the 58,000 service members who had died in Vietnam. Jack and Art had chosen a jury of renowned architects and artists to judge the competition, men whose professional stature could not be criticized. More than four hundred designs were submitted, and they were arrayed in an aircraft hangar at Andrews Air Force base near Washington DC, where the jury viewed them.

The design they finally selected was that of a young student at Yale who had proposed a V-shaped memorial of two black granite walls that sloped to a juncture below ground level. The names of the men and women who died in Vietnam were to be listed on the walls in the order in which they had died. One of the walls pointed directly at the Lincoln Memorial, the other at the Washington Memorial, well-known structures that rise in white splendor to honor our greatest national heroes. But the winning design was their exact opposite: it was black, not white, and it went down into the ground rather than up into the sky. How, I asked, did that "recognize and honor" Vietnam veterans?

Art and Jack had had no idea what design would win. But before they launched the design competition, they had chosen the first-class professional jury that made the final selection, and they would stand by its results, come what may. As it happened, however, they both just fell in love with the simple design that was selected.

Many Vietnam veterans, however, felt insulted by it. I was among them, and I asked to testify to that effect before the Fine Arts Commission, which had the final say on the design. But before giving my testimony, Art called me at home.

"Tom, I know you dislike the winning design, and that you are going to appear before the Fine Arts Commission to testify against it."

"That's true."

"Tom, listen to me. It has been a very tough fight for us just to get this far. You know that as well as I do, because I first got you involved in this, and a lot of us at VVMF worked hard on it—you, me, Jack Wheeler, Jan Scruggs, other people as well."

"Art, I just can't stand by and watch this happen."

"Well, Tom, stop for a moment and think about what you are about to do. We both know that there is a system involved in building a memorial in Washington. And now that a design has been selected by a first-class jury, I don't care if there is opposition, because when the Eiffel Tower was built, a lot of people just hated it. But a hundred years later, everyone thinks it's beautiful."

"Art, that's not the same."

"Tom, it's exactly the same! You may not like the design, but to me, the design is simple, elegant, unobtrusive, and, frankly, very beautiful. And that's the way art is—people will always disagree. But the members of the jury who made that selection are world-level experts and authorities, and if anyone could know what will be of enduring beauty on the Mall, it is them."

"I know, Art, but it's so . . . so . . ."

"What? You say it is the reverse of the Lincoln and Washington Memorials, but that's part of its beauty, don't you see? It is simple and elegant, a perfect way to memorialize our dead soldiers. You saw some of the designs that were submitted, everything from a giant helmet to a helicopter on a pole. If we didn't have this jury, we might have gotten some ugly monstrosity that would have permanently marred the Mall."

"Art, I just can't agree."

"Tom, you've got to try to get your emotions out of this. Those walls aren't some intentional insult to veterans, they are a silent, flowing design with no politics whatsoever. And like any other work of art, when they see it, visitors will think whatever they want to think."

"Art, neither of us are artists, and I still think it's ugly and offensive."

"Maybe you do, and maybe other people do as well. But a hundred years from now, the simple, elegant lines of those walls will be seen by future generations as one of the few good things that ever came out of the Vietnam War. So if you testify against the design and your protest wins, then all our work goes down the tube and you would wreck our whole effort."

"Art, that won't happen."

"Well, it very well could, that's the danger. So if you don't like the design, find one you do like, sell it to the American people, and get it built. Because that's what you'll have to do. And I know you don't agree with me, but I think the design truly is a very simple, flowing memorial of great and transcendent beauty."

I knew some people, even friends, thought I was a loud, obnoxious, and obstinate player, sometimes even a bit of a zealot for a poorly thought-out cause. Was that what I was doing here? I didn't know, and despite Art's counsel, I was already committed, so I testified.

After my appearance, the Fine Arts Commission approved the design chosen by the jury. But my opposition was echoed across the country, and it was followed by a year of brooding and shots fired by one side against the other in national newspapers and TV shows, including *60 Minutes*, on which both Art and I appeared.

I was supported by many people, including several members of Congress and Ross Perot, the wealthy Texan who is a Naval Academy graduate and later ran for president against Bush and Clinton in 1992. But VVMF was supported by many more important public figures, including senior generals, members of both houses of Congress, and many large corporations that spoke with their donations.

Throughout the controversy, Art stayed true to the cause, and he refuted some of the charges made by enemies of the design. No, black is not always the color of shame or sorrow, for both the Iwo Jima and the Sea Bee memorials are made of black granite. No, the memorial is not a gash cut into the ground, for the wall would be set into a hillside with a clear vista of the Mall. And no, the memorial was not a "V" mimicking the antiwar peace sign, for no human fingers could form a 125 degree "V."

The controversy was so strong that the secretary of the interior refused to let VVMF break ground on the Mall until they had resolved the differences expressed by the design's opponents. Senator John Warner of Virginia then hosted a compromise meeting between the two sides, which was heated. The ultimate agreement called for the addition of a statue of three soldiers wearing Vietnam-era uniforms and the addition of an American flag. With that agreement, Secretary Watt relented and the Vietnam Veterans Memorial was dedicated on March 26, 1982.

Thereafter, Art moved to Key West, where he worked with the local government. But his professional reputation was such that, in 1991, he was asked to run acquisition, development, and ultimate disposal of all sites used by the 1994 Olympic Games in Atlanta. Today he remains a worldwide authority on Olympic site issues, and in the first decade of the twenty-first century he spent a lot of time in Rio de Janeiro, basically filling the same role for the Olympic Games held there in 2016 that he had for the 1994 Olympics in Atlanta.

Life has been very good to Art. But in addition to his financial success, one of the great achievements of his life is the key role he played in the conception and construction of the Vietnam Veterans Memorial. And in 2014, as he predicted, that was the most visited memorial in the entire country.

Clearly, then, the American people have agreed with him rather than the memorial's opponents, a fact that can only give him enduring quiet satisfaction for a difficult mission accomplished under trying circumstances.

31

The Engineer

Bob Lowry took his commission in the Corps of Engineers, which, more than anything else, indicated that he was a very smart guy who loved the world of technical detail. He first spent two years as a lieutenant in Germany with his wife, Dotty, where his first two children were born. There he was assigned to an engineer construction battalion, which allowed him to cut his professional teeth. That was followed by a year in Vietnam, where he built bridges and other facilities with still another construction battalion, but this time as a captain with added authority and responsibility.

Upon his return to the United States, he earned two master's degrees in engineering from Stanford, then went back to West Point, where he taught engineering to Cadets from 1972 through 1976. For the next two years, he was the deputy director of public works at Fort Bliss, Texas, one of the largest army installations in the United States. His workforce consisted of 900 civilian employees charged with design, construction, operations, and maintenance of all facilities and infrastructure, which included 2.200 buildings, a major regional medical center, a jumbo-jet-capable airfield, and all associated utility and transportation systems.

That workload sounds overwhelming. But Bob took it on with relish, for he loved nothing more than construction, and the more complicated, the better. In many ways, he filled the role of an ideal West Point graduate in the army: smart, tough, reliable, resilient, and highly competent in his chosen professional field. And the army saw his skills and made use of them.

From 1981 through 1984, for instance, he was the program manager for the U.S. Army's operations and facility maintenance in the Republic of Korea. In that role, he developed and executed design programs and managed construction with an in-place value of more than $250 million annually. And the beat kept on: from 1984 through 1986, Bob was the director of public works at Fort Leavenworth, Kansas. As such, he was responsible for operations, maintenance, and repair of all facilities and infrastructure, including military housing, a community hospital, a military prison, a military airfield, and all related utility and transportation infrastructure, including a central heating plant and a water treatment facility.

Over the next several years, Bob was the director and head of the department of military engineering at the U.S. Army School at Fort Belvoir, Virginia. And over the early eighties, his reputation as an engineer had grown by leaps and bounds, such that in 1986 he was named the Federal Engineer of the Year by the National Society of Professional Engineers. Other such awards would accumulate, but he kept his eye on the ball, and he flourished.

From 1989 through 1991, Bob found himself back at Fort Leavenworth, but this time as the garrison commander (city manager equivalent). Fort Leavenworth was a military community with some 15,000 residents, and he was the senior operating manager of a staff of more than 1,200 civilian employees and 200 military personnel, who staffed the departments of human resources, public works, fire control, law enforcement, procurement, supply and equipment maintenance, and parks and community activities.

In that role, he developed and executed an annual operating budget in excess of $100 million. While he was in command, the Fort Leavenworth garrison was twice selected, in 1989 and 1991, as the best medium-sized army installation in the United States, based on quality of facilities and services.

In 1991 Bob retired from the army as a colonel and immediately became the director of public works for the city of Leavenworth, Kansas, a full-service community of 40,000 residents. In that role, he was responsible for the operations of the street, wastewater, refuse, and fleet maintenance divisions, and for all personnel and budgetary aspects of the department. From 1993 through 2004, he held similar positions of ever-increasing responsibilities in Lenexa followed by Overland Park, Kansas.

While working there, Bob was selected by the American Public Works Association (APWA) to be a Top 10 Public Works Leader of the year 2000, and in 2003 he was awarded the Distinguished Service Award by the Design-Built Institute of America. This was a result of his work as project manager for a new convention center and hotel for the City of Overland Park. Both projects came in ahead of schedule and under budget, neither of which happens too often on government jobs.

In 2004 Bob was named the director of public works for Arlington, Texas, a full-service community of more than 350,000 residents and home of the Texas Rangers baseball team, the Six Flags Over Texas amusement park, and the University of Texas at Arlington. Shortly thereafter, the voters of Arlington approved a sales tax levy to assist Jerry Jones in the construction of his new stadium ("Jerry's World") and Bob was heavily involved in that project, mostly in getting the public infrastructure—roads, water, sewer, etc.—built to support the stadium. Then in 2011 Bob was named a Fellow in the American Public Works Association, and he remains active in that organization to the present day. In fact, unlike most of his peers, the one thing Bob wants to find under his Christmas tree is a massive public works project that is both badly needed and finds itself in serious trouble, such that he is needed to come flying in to the rescue. And he only hopes for such an opportunity to come again, for that's what he has done best of all during his entire adult career as a public works engineer.

32

Pension Asset Management

On June 8, 1966, Mike Mewhinney graduated from West Point, was commissioned a second lieutenant in the U.S. Army Signal Corps, and married his high school sweetheart, Linda. After his service as a communications officer in Vietnam, Mike left the army and earned an MBA from Harvard. He then went to work with Goldman Sachs in Dallas as an institutional sales-man, and within a few years he was a vice president.

The middle and late seventies saw a certain amount of change within the financial services industry. For instance, after the 1976 passage of the Employees Retirement Income Security Act, or ERISA, large corporations were often uncertain what steps to take in order to prudently comply with that law. Choosing a careful and conservative path, they usually employed consul-tants to help them choose managers for their pension plans. In fact, statistics show that during the 1980s, roughly 95 percent of all manager searches were assisted by consultants.

From the late seventies into the early eighties, then, pension fund management was in a somewhat fluid state. One of Mike's major clients at Goldman Sachs was the trust department at Republic Bank. But Mike is a very personable guy, so in addi-tion to business, he had become close friends with three trust officers there, particularly the director of the trust department, Jim Barrow. They became so close, in fact, that Mike was best man at Jim's wedding and was the godfather of his first child.

Many bankers were well aware of the presentations being made to corporate boards by would-be money managers, mostly those associated with big banks from other cities. And while these dog-and-pony shows often met with success, Mike and his three friends from Republic, Barrow, Hanley & Strauss, were unimpressed. If the occasion ever arose, they agreed, they would be able to make much more impressive and promising proposals. But in the scheme of things, stasis won yet again, and so the four of them all stayed at their very highly paid positions at Goldman Sachs and at Republic Bank.

Then, in the summer of 1979, lightning struck: Hanley, as often happened at big banks in those days, and for no apparent reason, was fired by Republic Bank. At first this was a shock. But soon enough, the four of them agreed that this would be their opportunity to get into the business of managing corporate pension assets. So Mike and the other two officers in the trust department at Republic all quit their jobs to go into business together. They formed the alphabetically ordered company of Barrow, Hanley, Mewhinney & Strauss (BHM&S), leased office space, and immediately started promoting their business.

This was a big risk for all four, of course, so none of them drew salaries, and they saved wherever they could—Hanley's wife, Nancy, for instance, was their secretary and office manager while they cold-called corporate boards and banks, basically dialing for dollars.

At the time, most retirement funds were being managed by big banks in New York, and there were not many other individuals out on the street offering the same services as did Mike's company. But all four of them had excellent records and reputations within the financial community. Because of that, within six months they were able to secure management of a portion of Phillips Petroleum's pension assets. But a year went by with no more management contracts coming in, and things started to get tight. In fact, with no success after Phillips Petroleum, it wasn't long before Mike felt like they were floundering.

Given their records, all four of them were eminently rehireable by big Dallas banks. But this was their high-risk shot at significant power in the financial services industry, and none of them were ready, quite yet, to quit. So they beavered away, confident that they would make it if they stuck to their guns. And at the time, all they had to pay the rent and keep the lights on was their small income stream from management of a very minor portion of Phillips pension assets.

By the spring of 1981, after having been in business for eighteen months, things were really looking glum. For the first time, all four of them were thinking about giving up and going back into banking. Then, in 1981, Mike went to our fifteenth class reunion at West Point.

Mike enjoyed himself immensely, and while there, he ran into Dick Graff from the class of 1971. Dick was long out of the army, both were from Texas, and the two of them really hit it off. It turned out that Dick lived in Houston, where he was a senior officer at one of the biggest pension consultant companies in the country. Dick had vaguely heard of BHM&S, but because of their common background, he invited Mike to come to Houston and pitch their firm.

Mike did so, and he and Graff became even closer friends. While that visit did not result in any immediate contracts, the most important thing Mike learned from Dick was how to navigate the hoops and hurdles of various consultant companies. Back in Dallas, Mike shared that information with his partners, and they went back to work. And soon enough, *mirabile dictu*, they were being invited by big corporations to make presentations of their pension asset management skills, and contracts started to fall in their laps.

In fact, between 1984 and 1986 they made thirty-three "final" presentations to corporate boards. Of that number, they were awarded thirty contracts to manage pension assets, including nineteen in a row. By 1985 they had established a formidable reputation within their industry, and by the end of 1986 they were managing $5 billion in assets. They typically earned an annual income for this service of four-tenths of 1 percent of the amount they managed, which came out, by the end of 1986, to roughly $20 million. Of course, that amount is split among four partners, and they also have to pay for office space and other overhead. Even so, that's a nice annual income.

After 1986 they did very well with the funds entrusted to them, which meant that their income continued to grow substantially. This growth came not only from new clients who wanted in on their success, but also from enlargement of the assets they managed for clients already in the fold. Federal Express, for instance, started in 1985 by entrusting $15 million to their care, and ten years later, in 1996, their account was $2 billion. And the corporations whose pension assets they managed were quite sizable, including General Motors, Johnson & Johnson, and American Airlines.

In 1999 the assets managed by BHM&S had grown to $60 billion. For Mike, building the business in the early days had been not only profitable but also a lot of fun. But by the late nineties he decided that his partnership had turned into little more than a job. So, after twenty years as a partner, he retired and invested his assets elsewhere.

The most famous West Point graduates are those who rose to general officer, fought our battles, and won our wars. If asked, these men would doubtless say that much of their success came from what they had learned as West Point Cadets.

Although his time in uniform was brief, Mike has not forgotten from whence he sprung, and so has long given large donations to West Point. For instance, in 2012 he was the only donor who gave more than $10 million to the academy. He has long since become the largest donor to West Point in history, with hundreds of millions more promised to USMA from his estate. Although he never made general officer, to the people who keep the books at West Point, Mike's star shines very brightly indeed.

33

Saving Apple's Cookies

After Vietnam, Deme Clainos earned a master's in computer engineering and a master's in marketing from the University of Arizona, then went to work for Hewlett Packard in the early 1970s. But with the great mobility within the computer industry, he found himself in Cupertino, California, working for Apple in the early 1980s. After several years of progressively increasing responsibility, he was made director of direct sales, which included all of Apple's engagement with small businesses, education, and value-added resellers.

Two years after he had taken on that prestigious post, in the spring of 1984, he was called up to the office of Apple's president and CEO, John Scully.

When Deme walked into his office, Scully stood up and came around his desk to shake his hand. But they weren't alone, because stretched out on the couch looking at him was Steve Jobs, the brains and the power inside Apple. Deme had met and dealt with both, but he still didn't know what this meeting was about. He started small talk with Scully, but was soon interrupted by Jobs.

"Deme, let's get to the heart of things. IBM is eating our lunch in corporate America."

Apple was pushing their PC, known as Apple II, to their corporate clients, but IBM had come out with the IBM PC, and the Apple business with corporate America had all but disappeared.

IBM had been producing big computers for so long that they basically had the corporate market sewn up. All big companies started with big IBM computers down the hall somewhere, so when they came out with their PC, suddenly every worker bee had a personal computer on his desk, and he didn't have to go down the hall anymore to get his work done. But these IBM PCs were all interconnected. And that meant that Apple, as well as all of the other non-IBMs with none of the interconnectivity required by big business, was basically dead in the water.

Jobs continued.

"We still have sales to small businesses, schools, and so on, but we were basically locked out of big business because of this interconnectivity issue."

John Scully spoke up.

"And remember, Deme, eventually, small business will not buy what big business has rejected."

Deme knew all this, of course—everyone at Apple did.

"Okay. So what do you want me to do?"

Steve Jobs smiled.

"Deme, I know we've talked about this before. And if I remember correctly, you like sixties music almost as much as I do, right?"

Deme laughed. "Yeah, I think so."

"And you like Joan Baez?"

"Do I like her? I bought all her albums, I love listening to her voice, she's the greatest!"

"Well, one of her best songs, in my opinion, is 'It's All Over Now, Baby Blue.' Do you know it?"

"Sure."

"Good. Well, in the song, no one knows who 'Baby Blue' was meant to be. But we *all* know who 'Big Blue' is—IBM! Now, we don't want to overdo this, but obviously, our goal is to be a major player in the corporate market. We chose you to help us with this from among a half-dozen or so individuals because of your creativity and marketing skills. And if you agree to take this project on, that's going to be your target. Our people seem just overwhelmed by Big Blue, and even though our products may even be superior to those of IBM, we just can't make our voice heard in the marketplace. Last year, our sales to corporate clients were only about a half-million dollars, and that's way less than 1 percent of what big corporations spend in this market. So Deme, if you agree to undertake this project, we want you to choose a dozen or two people you know within our organization, and we want you to take them to some offsite location and have a basic open-ended think tank. Meet every day and talk about this, research it, write about it, whatever you want. But your goal will be to propose ways in which Apple will be able to enter the corporate marketplace in a big way. Basically, we want you to tell us how we're going to catch up with and then surpass IBM. What do you think?"

Deme shrugged. This was quite a challenge. And if he failed, it looked like that would be it for him. Even as a senior corporate officer at Apple, he knew he would be under quite a cloud of failure and would probably end up leaving Apple. But anybody can do the easy stuff, so he was intrigued, to say the least.

"Sure, I'll do it. At least I will know what my goal is, however elusive that may be."

"Great! Now you think about this for a while, talk to your colleagues, and when you have gotten fifteen or twenty people to join you on this quest, we'll get you some offsite office space for as long as you need it. Tell the people you take with you that I said they would get regular increases in salary, stock options, whatever else we can come up with. I will do my best to see that they don't lose any ground while they're doing this, and that goes for you as well. But for Apple, this project will become our first priority until you have either come up with a plan to overcome this interconnectivity and marketing promotion problem or decided to abandon the chase. We'll give you as much time as you need, but I'd like you to check in with us every few months, just to see how you're doing. We don't expect magic out of you, and it may well be that there's no real answer to our problem. But Deme, it looks to me like a big marketing challenge, and that's where you shine. And John and I agree that if anyone on our payroll can figure this out, you're the man."

Deme was quick to respond.

"Well, Steve, if that's what you want, then the first thing we want to do at Apple is stop talking about IBM and their products. Our mission should be to serve the corporate customer, to give them the right hardware and software to do their jobs better than they have been done before. We don't have to argue our case against IBM with them, just let our equipment do what it does, that's all. And we're not competing with IBM here. Rather, we are competing to please our customer, and so the name 'IBM,' or any of their products, need never be mentioned here at Apple again. And if I had any say in the matter, that would mean from this moment forward."

Jobs was grinning.

"Deme, I like the way you think, and what you just said will be gospel here. From now on, I don't want to hear IBM or any of their products mentioned at Apple again. John, get that word out today."

Deme had been in this business for more than ten years, and he knew a lot of people, both within and outside of Apple. So over the following weeks, he invited eighteen people to join him in this project. To them, this certainly sounded exciting, and if they were able to succeed, why, they could transform the entire Apple world.

But it was also a risk, and despite whatever Steve Jobs said, while working on this project they would be out of the chain of command and operating more or less on their own, and group failure meant personal failure. Because of that, only fourteen agreed to join him, and of that number, Deme decided within the first few weeks that two of them just didn't fit. So eventually, it was Deme and his twelve apostles holed up in a remote area of Apple.

After two months, they seemed to make a breakthrough, and they spent another month refining it. Then, just short of four months after they began, Deme was satisfied that they had a deliverable product that would completely change the ways in which Apple did business. Because of the ways they set it up, this approach seemed almost to guarantee them a shot at big corporate accounts. So when Deme made his presentation to Steve Jobs and John Scully, they were simply delighted.

To launch the new plan, Apple invited all the regional operating groups, several corporate groups, and all the senior executives to come to a three-day conference in Cupertino and learn the new marketing approach arrived at by Deme and the Twelve. The word had been put out months earlier that Apple employees everywhere in the country and around the world were not to talk about IBM's interconnectivity or Apple's lack of it. They were told, in no uncertain terms, to come to the meeting and not to talk about IBM's threat, but rather to learn how Apple planned to win corporate America.

Before the first day of the heavily promoted conference arrived, it had once again been emphasized to all Apple invitees that any mention of IBM's interconnectivity products was strictly forbidden. Deme gave the opening speech to a crowd of several hundred, and the conference schedule was filled with one- and two-hour classes in which Apple employees would learn the new ways in which they could realistically expect to win big contracts with corporate clients. Deme didn't want to waste any time, and after he had finished his introductory speech, a hand came up in the middle of the audience. He really didn't want to deal with questions at this point, but everyone else saw the hand raised, so he called on him. A portly, balding man stood up.

"I'm Joe Smith from Cleveland. Before we go any further, I just want to clear one thing up. When we have finished these three days and we go home, will we then be able to match IBM's interconnectivity products we're trying to compete with?"

Before he could answer, a voice came from the rear of the crowd.

"Deme, I'll answer that."

It was Bill Campbell, Apple's executive vice president for sales and marketing, and there was a rustling in the crowd as he made his way forward. Then he mounted the stage with Deme and turned to the audience.

"Whoever asked that question, could I hear it again? And please state your name and where you're from clearly."

"Yes, my name is Joe Smith from Cleveland, and I asked if, when we go home at the end of this conference, would we be able to compete with those IBM interconnectivity products."

"Okay, Mister Smith, that's what I thought you said. You obviously have not been reading anything we have been sending you about our new approach to corporations, or you just don't care. Either way, you're fired. Leave immediately, someone will meet you outside, but there won't be another word spoken until you are gone."

There were a few minutes of utter silence while Joe Smith struggled with his briefcase and papers. But then he was gone and Bill asked the crowd if there were any more questions.

There were not.

So the three days of classes proceeded as planned, and the conference itself was a great success, bringing Deme and his team a standing ovation at the final meeting. And the new approach that had been learned by all the operational groups was implemented immediately. By year's end, annual corporate sales had grown from $500,000 to over $12 million; by the next year, $40 million; and during the following year, sales had skyrocketed again. But by that time, Deme had left Apple and started his own company in Portland, Oregon.

Such movement between computer companies was really quite common at the time, and before leaving Apple, of course, Deme had been amply rewarded with stock options and such.

During his last year at Apple, Deme and his wife, Diane,

joined several hundred Apple employees at the annual Apple Christmas party. It was definitely a festive occasion, with everyone laughing and chattering gaily, for once again, it had been a very good year for Apple. A big band was playing and many of the couples were dancing.

Deme and Diane soon found their place cards on a table, and they were quickly caught up in the gaiety. But they had not been there more than ten minutes when the orchestra suddenly stopped playing. A silence came over the crowd, and Deme and Diane could see people moving aside in front of them, as if someone had entered the room and was moving toward them. Then the final few people moved aside, and Deme saw that it was Steve Jobs moving his way. But he could see that Steve was holding someone's hand, pulling the person along behind him, though he couldn't see who it was. Then Steve spoke:

"Deme, I'd like you to meet Joan Baez."

Joan Baez? Then Steve pulled his arm forward and there she was, in the flesh. Deme couldn't breathe as he looked at her. My god! Steve Jobs's date is Joan Baez!

"Deme, Steve has told me so much about you and what you've done for Apple! Would you like to dance?"

34

Taking Baghdad

After leaving the army, I earned a law degree from the University of Michigan, worked in Amsterdam, Los Angeles, Brussels, and Washington D C, earned a PhD in history from Princeton, and wrote a number of military history books. In 1997 I got a top literary agent, which allowed me to quit my "day job" and write full time.

One of my good friends in Washington was Duncan Hunter, who, like me, had been an infantry platoon leader in Vietnam. Duncan was a congressman from San Diego, and we became friends while working on a Vietnam veterans issue in the early eighties. He was on the House Armed Services Committee, and periodically I would visit him on Capitol Hill.

I made such a visit on Wednesday, March 26, 2003. At that time U.S. forces were fighting in Iraq, driving toward the capital city of Baghdad, which they were about to surround. By then, Duncan had become chairman of the House Armed Services Committee, and he shared with me some of his concerns. The most important one was the threat of ever higher casualties among U.S. soldiers and Marines who would be fighting to take Baghdad.

As we talked, I told Duncan that I knew some people with the right backgrounds—maybe we could come up with some ideas for taking Baghdad with fewer casualties by, say, Monday?

On Saturday, March 29, a dozen old friends came to my home

to help me. During the early afternoon, we searched for a historical model of a besieged city that had been taken with few casualties. The wooden horse left outside the gates of Troy was an obvious but rare success, with the fate of most such cities usually turning on how long they could endure the siege. Within a few hours, we seemed to find ourselves coming to a dead end.

At the time I was writing a book about the Civil War (*Lost Triumph*, Putnam, 2005), and it turned out that both Judge Gene Sullivan and several others in our group, including military historian Jim Yarrison and retired generals Bill Richardson and Nick Krawciw, had spent much of their professional lives studying and even trying to implement lessons they had learned from the Civil War. So by Saturday afternoon, we had begun walking through Dixie verbally and with textbooks, looking for besieged cities, towns, or positions that had been taken with few casualties on either side. And the best example we found was the way Sherman had taken Atlanta.

On August 31, 1864, Sherman sent a large element of his Union Army to the southwestern side of Atlanta in an effort to cut the last two railroad lines into that city. The Confederates were outmanned and thoroughly whipped, and after they had retreated at nightfall, Sherman sent a fresh corps of twelve thousand men up the now-undefended rail line into the heart of Atlanta. When the sun came up on September 1, blue soldiers were occupying the train station in the city center and were pouring down central streets. Confederate general Hood realized his elaborate defenses had been penetrated, and he decided to abandon Atlanta with his army.

So it was clearly possible to maneuver an army out of a city, as had been done 140 years earlier. But with the dramatically improved weapons and equipment on both sides in 2003, the question remained how we could do that in Baghdad.

We knew we had to come up with an idea not considered by men in uniform—some audacious, daring, bold stroke, which was highly improbable from within the army. That's not because they're not smart, but simply because of bureaucracy: proposal of a high-risk move might well be a chance for victory. But it would also be a risk of failure, and thus of professional humiliation for the commander. With little doubt, then, any such proposal would have been shot down by someone superior to the planner(s), playing his staff role of protecting those above him from risk. Thus it is that most truly bold plans predictably die before ever reaching the top.

So what would our truly bold plan be?

There was an area in the heart of Baghdad by a big bend in the Euphrates where one of Saddam Hussein's palaces was located. Nearby were the Revolutionary Command Council that ran the country, the National Assembly, the Iraqi intelligence service, and the Iraqi Supreme Court. We named this "Capitol Hill, Baghdad," and it became the focus of our attention.

Though we were all talking around it, Gene Sullivan, the chief judge of a federal appeals court and a former tanker himself, was the first to suggest a bold armored strike into the heart of Baghdad. Just as Sherman had sent that fresh corps into the heart of Atlanta, Gene said an armored column should move in, down the same massive highways we had built for them, then occupy the Iraqi government's vital organs and essentially shut it down. No Iraqi troops would be prepared to defend the city center, and the shock and surprise of this completely unexpected stab into Baghdad's heart by American tanks should paralyze resistance.

But retired general Nick Krawciw had a concern.

During the Yom Kippur War in 1973, Nick had been an observer with the Israeli Defense Force. On October 23 the Israeli command tried to take Suez City with an armored brigade. But from upper floors of buildings, Egyptian soldiers fired rocket-propelled grenades (RPGs) down on Israeli tanks passing below. These blew through the thin armor on the tank tops, thus killing engines and/or crew members. Israeli soldiers abandoned their vehicle hulks, and the result was a major Israeli defeat. Nick's warning, then, was that if we ran a column of tanks into Baghdad, they might meet the same embarrassing failure at the hands of Saddam Hussein's RPG wielders.

So how would we get around that potential trap?

Jim Yarrison, who held a PhD from Princeton in Middle Eastern studies, suggested we do what the Germans had done in 1940 when they took Eben-Emael, a huge L-shaped Belgian stone fortress at the intersection of a major canal and the Meuse River. Bristling with guns that covered both water courses, it seemed an impregnable defense against any German invasion.

But this barrier was crucially important to Hitler, and he decided to take it by glider assault. On the night of May 10, 1940, a specially trained force of 78 German engineers in ten gliders landed on the roof of the Eben-Emael fortress. Using shaped charges, they blew through the stone and steel defenses and won the surrender of the 1,200-man garrison without a shot fired.

So Jim suggested that the U.S. Army use helicopters to transport soldiers onto "Capitol Hill, Baghdad" at night. Their surprise arrival would meet little resistance, and they would easily take all the important buildings. Most of us (two holdouts) agreed on recommending this bold attack.

The report I wrote Sunday night, March 30, consisted of four single-spaced pages and two maps. On Monday morning, Gene Sullivan, Jim Yarrison, and I went to Duncan Hunter's office and presented to him our ideas on how to take Baghdad with little loss of American life. Hunter was impressed, and he invited us back to his office that afternoon to give the same presentation to a half-dozen other members of the House Armed Services Committee. They seemed pleased, and that night we were called at home and asked to come to Hunter's office the next morning at 9 a.m. to brief Gen. Richard Myers, the chairman of the Joint Chiefs of Staff.

Next morning, the three of us did so, followed by General Myers's questions. He asked if he could have the maps and papers, then said he would get them to American commanders in Iraq. Duncan was confident they would use our ideas, but no one knew.

The following Sunday, April 5, I saw a clip on the news showing what was first called a raid to test Iraqi defenses, but which the army later called a "Thunder Run." This was a column of American armored vehicles that smashed into Baghdad from the south, cruised along its main avenues, then crashed back out of town on its western side. Two days later, another Thunder Run was launched from the south, but instead of exiting to the west, this armored column went straight north and took Capitol Hill, Baghdad. Within hours, news footage showed American tanks and dismounted soldiers surrounding the palace and other central governmental buildings.

We were a bit disappointed that they hadn't used our idea for helicopter assault. But, hey, we won, and U.S. forces were occupying the city! From the early footage on television, it looked like Saddam Hussein's forces were crumbling and fighting would soon end. Then Hunter's secretary called, inviting me, Sullivan, Yarrison, and some others to come to his office.

When we got there, the T V showed American tanks pulling down a big black statue of Saddam Hussein in a public square. Duncan was all smiles as he pointed to the television screen.

"You guys know, and I know, that a lot of this may have come from your ideas."

We were incredulous, even openly laughing. He chuckled with us, but he was serious.

"No, no, really. I watched you brief your proposal to General Myers, the chairman of the Joint Chiefs, who then took your materials and said he would send them to the U.S. command in Iraq. So your ideas were seriously considered at the highest levels. Now, originally, we had been planning to take Baghdad the same way the Brits had just taken Basra—like unpeeling an onion a layer at a time, with house-to-house, street-to-street fighting, and so on. But you said we should avoid getting hung up that way, that we should just charge right onto Capitol Hill, Baghdad, and kill the enemy force there. And that's what we did. You said we should use helicopters, we used tanks, but to the same end: with one bold stroke, we took and held the heart of the city."

As the statue on TV came crashing down, cheers erupted. Then Duncan continued: "So who ordered that attack? You would expect important orders like that to come from above, which is why I think those planning staffs may have used your ideas. But for all we know, it could have been the commander of that second Thunder Run who just decided on his own to attack into city center, with no outside input. But either way, you should still be proud, for great minds think alike, and that strike took Capitol Hill, Baghdad, and won the war!"

Wow, that sounded great! We all cheered spontaneously, suddenly giddy again. Even from so far away, we wanted to contribute something. And though we suspected our ideas had not been used, the army staffs were so big that you never knew. You just never knew . . .

"I spoke to General Myers earlier, and he asked me to thank you once again for your ideas about taking Baghdad. But we all know that victories have a thousand fathers, so there is little chance you will ever get any public credit for this. In fact, let's be honest—there's no chance at all. However, you've gotten the thanks of the chairman of the House Armed Services Committee and the chairman of the Joint Chiefs of Staff. And given politics, I'm afraid that's all the thanks you're going to get. Even so, sleep well tonight, guys, for a job well done."

35

Rocket Man

After graduation, Mike Brennan did marry Medea, or Helen, the Wisconsin farmer's daughter who was wed as a mythic heroine.

Thereafter, Mike went to flight school, then flew fixed wing aircraft in Vietnam for a year. Upon his return, he went to graduate school at Stanford for two years and got a master's degree in aeronautical engineering, then began to teach at West Point in the department of earth, space, and graphic sciences. By this time, Mike and Helen had three children and a fourth was on the way. But all of a sudden, his lifelong dream looked like a real possibility, so he and Helen had a long heart-to-heart talk about their future.

All his life Mike had wanted to be an astronaut, and while at Stanford he had applied to NASA and been put on "hold" until he finished his degrees. Then someone at NASA gave him an inside tip, but strictly "off the record." He was told that if, in addition to his aeronautical degrees, Mike got a medical degree, he would be a shoo-in to be chosen by NASA to become an astronaut.

Mike then had a very secure post as a major teaching at West Point, a great family environment, a wonderful place to raise kids. And if he played his cards right, he could see himself ending up at West Point, some years down the line, as a permanent professor. To any of his West Point classmates, that would be considered an enviable outcome. But the dream of one day walking on the moon just wouldn't leave him alone.

So hearing of the advantage an MD degree would give him in the NASA competition to become an astronaut, he quickly learned that he could go to medical school under a special army program. But the catch was that, in order for the army to pay for his medical school, he had to be reduced in rank to second lieutenant, the lowest, and lowest-paying commissioned officer grade, the same lowly rank he had first obtained after graduation from West Point.

With three children already arrived and a fourth on the way, this could be a big problem for all of them, but especially for Helen. They clearly couldn't get by as a family on a second lieutenant's pay, and that could only mean that, while he was in medical school for four years, she would have to go back to work as a nurse.

Mike was already thirty years old, supposedly the unwritten cutoff age for applicants to medical school. Suppose he didn't like medical school, what would they do then? He thought that he probably would have been allowed to return to West Point and teach again. But after switching from flying airplanes in the army to teaching at West Point to washing out of medical school, that final failure to thrive would be a major career blow. So should they even risk it?

Mike was a bit hesitant as he laid things out for Helen, because it would all depend on her taking on a great burden for four years. This was obviously a very high risk venture, and they both would have to lay it all on the line: their family future would depend on his ability to earn a medical degree while Helen supported them.

But to his great delight, Helen was very matter-of-fact about the whole thing: "All right, where do you want to go to medical school?"

Mike's boss at West Point was Col. Gilbert Kirby, a strictly by-the-book commander who was hard as nails and tolerated no performance short of flawless. But when Mike went to him and asked for help in getting into the special army program for medical school, he suddenly turned into a big teddy bear.

Mike ended up at the University of Texas, and sure enough, for his four years of medical school he was a second lieutenant. And as a nurse, Helen brought in much more money than he did. Once he had received his MD degree, Mike reapplied to NASA and spent a week or so with NASA's famous Ground Control in Houston getting tested, prodded, poked, and grilled.

The news came a few weeks later, and to his great surprise Mike did not make the final cut. When he heard that news he was already in specialty training in ophthalmology, though the fantasy of becoming an astronaut still filled his dreams. He was a bit crestfallen, therefore, at having been rejected as a potential astronaut.

But Helen was simply delighted. She had never restricted his dreams, and did not then. But the thought of her superbly educated husband blasting off on a rocket was ridiculous, an almost-silly nonsensical nightmare. And now that he had finally been rejected by NASA, she finally told him how much she had been frightened by his becoming an astronaut.

So Mike made his career as an army doctor and traveled quite a bit over twenty-odd years. When he and Helen finally retired, it was to a small community in North Carolina, where he now continues to practice medicine. But he also has kept intact the professional connections he had established over the years. Since his retirement from the U.S. Army, he has been hired as a consultant by the Department of Defense to help set up ophthalmology clinics in medical schools inside both Iraq and Afghanistan, which he has done over numerous visits to those countries.

But independent of his army career and military connections, Mike has also developed a remarkable array of professional contacts around the world. And he has used those contacts to develop a program of leadership development for young medical professionals of around thirty years of age, men and women who will, one day, become their nations' medical leaders.

Mike has installed and developed this leadership program in

the capitals as well as many smaller cities inside the countries of Vietnam, Thailand, the Philippines, Kuala Lumpur, Syria, Lebanon, Yemen, Egypt, and Libya.

Medea was able to distract the Marines while Jason and his cohorts stole the Golden Fleece. And she went along with risking their professional future by working to support her second lieutenant husband and their four children for four years. But now, at long last, the high-risk times were behind them. And, best of all, she would never have to endure watching her husband shoot into space on a volcano-like mountain of flame.

No, he hadn't attained that lifelong dream of becoming an astronaut. But he had become a medical doctor, and all in all, Mike and Helen have done very well indeed.

They are as happy today as anyone has any right to be.

As are we Argonauts all.

Other Works by Tom Carhart

Battles and Campaigns in Vietnam (Crown, 1984)

The Offering (Morrow, 1987)

Iron Soldiers (Pocket Books, 1994)

West Point Warriors (Warner Books, 2002)

Still Loyal Be (Betimpress, 2003)

Lost Triumph (G. P. Putnam's Sons, 2005)

A Time to Lead by Gen. Wesley K Clark (Ret.) and Tom Carhart (Palgrave Macmillan, 2008)

Sacred Ties (Berkeley Caliber, 2010)